D0627747

The Adventures
of Form and Content

Also by Albert Goldbarth

The Adventures of Form and Content

ESSAYS

Albert
Goldbarth

GRAYWOLF PRESS

This publication is made possible, in part, by the voters of Minnesota through a Minnesota State Arts Board Operating Support grant, thanks to a legislative appropriation from the arts and cultural heritage fund, and through a grant from the Wells Fargo Foundation. Significant support has also been provided by Target, the McKnight Foundation, the Amazon Literary Partnership, and other generous contributions from foundations, corporations, and individuals. To these organizations and individuals we offer our heartfelt thanks.

Published by Graywolf Press
250 Third Avenue North, Suite 600
Minneapolis, Minnesota 55401

www.graywolfpress.org

Published in the United States of America

ISBN 978-1-55597-761-0

2 4 6 8 9 7 5 3 1
First Graywolf Printing, 2017

Library of Congress Control Number: 2016938022

Cover design: Kyle G. Hunter

CONTENTS

This train carries saints and sinners
This train carries losers and winners
This train carries whores and gamblers
. . . All aboard.
  // BRUCE SPRINGSTEEN, "Land of Hope and Dreams"

"All of us have one sort of speech for the vicar and
another for the man who pumps the gas."
  // JANET BURROWAY, *Writing Fiction*

The Adventures
of Form and Content

Annals of Absence

1.

One looks like the side of a boxcar: flat; rectangular; russet; and so the spots on its body are passable for graffiti. One, and another one nearby, look like experiments in italicized calligraphy. In the spell of a torch's flickering, some seem to have the motion of tattoos on flexing muscles. But the fact is that our metaphors and modifiers fail: the beauty and mystery of the cave art animals obviously precede—and are forever beyond—our verbal decoration.

The images in Chauvet Cave are thirty-two thousand years old, "four times as long as recorded history," Judith Thurman points out. Our own world changes with dizzying rapidity: my grandmother's life included Kitty Hawk at one end, *Sputnik* at the other, and that was before the weekly reinvention of Internet technofashions and the wham-bam jump-cut pace of music videos. But for thirty-two thousand years the aurochs and stags and ibex and bison and horses and mammoths were created in the dangerous dark of caves in Spain and France with a consistency of look that makes their passage through the Aurignacian, Gravettian, Solutrean, and Magdalenian seamless; makes a single bestiary that has no need of change.

Increasingly, fewer of us will ever stand in the caves in front of them, although splendid books of photographs exist and, recently, Werner Herzog's film of Chauvet. Whoever *has* (through chance, in the beginning; today, through bureaucratic permission) entered that hidden world of stone and dark, and stood there human-face-to-unhuman-face, records a transcendent experience, "holy," "unearthly"; words like "power," "vitality," "grace" are common, often in a context that admits how sadly inadequate they are. These animals have a culminant *hereness* that we rarely find in their cousins at the zoo—or in our neighbors or, if we really have to put it this way, in our selves.

I'm thinking today about absence. It might be, at least in part, that a bison's imposing grandeur is so intense *because,* as Thurman puts it, "nothing of the landscape—clouds, earth, sun, moon, rivers, or plant life, and, only rarely, a horizon—figures in cave art." These are some of "many striking omissions," she tells us. Maybe it's *because* "no human conflict is recorded in cave art," and because the artists (would they have *thought of themselves* as "artists"?) "rarely chose to depict human beings," that the two does are so daintily imperial, and the lion says he will never yield to time, and the *Megaloceros* stag is as much at home in our brains as are their own convolutions. Maybe these animals seem so "here" because they feed on everything else that isn't, the way the dancing flame fed on the lump of grease in the stone lamps they were painted by, and the way we cling to one another, wicking up the universe of dark matter that surrounds us.

Absence . . . I look at my hand, *this* hand that's writing with a Bic pen in an everyday dime-store notebook, and was scraped along its outer edge when it tried to brace against a fall the other day (it looks like gray-tinged bacon), and was tended to by my wife, with soap and water, antiseptic cream, a Band-Aid, and a touch of spousal sympathy from *her* hand, just as light as a moth-wing's brush. However, I've read enough in lay texts on twentieth-century physics to know that between the atoms, and *in* the atoms, this hand is mainly empty air: a tiny spritz of elements held in an overwhelming void. The same for a two-by-four, of course, a pitted meteorite, an I-beam, a tusk. But human flesh . . . ? Yes, human flesh: a whiffle of "me" in a framework filled by absolute dead-on zero.

2.

Peggy Rabb was my colleague for a year, and now she's gone. I've heard those same words, "power," "vitality," "grace," applied to her, too. And her impish sense of humor. And the flea-market finds she begifted throughout the sixth floor, for no reason except her joy in life, to full professors and secretaries alike; I got a blue mesh bag of 1950s turquoise plastic typewriter keys. She bolted down bourbon and belted out hymns and limericks. Everyone misses her. Or everyone (it's an English department, after all) who wasn't secretly envious of her effortless charm. A year later, her name remains on her office door. I'm thinking today about absence.

How that door is such a *real,* knockable, tape-a-note-onable, solid thing—and floats, like the ocher rhinos of prehistoric caves, on a field of absence. How we all walk every day, all day, through unlimited meadows of emptiness: what happens between the toggled switch and the lightbulb's watting to life, what line of transmission exists between the turn-on keystroke and the lit screen, or between the turned ignition key and the engine thrum. That's Dimension X for myself and my friends. Most of us still live in a world of magic.

For an in-class essay one afternoon, a woman gilds her idea— that poets sometimes "juggle time"—with a fannish pop reference to *Star Trek.* As you probably know, the crew of the *Next Generation* series livens up its tedious travel through empty space by playing on the holodeck, having adventures with, say, characters from the Sherlock Holmes stories. "Holydeck," she's written. It's a charming misconception—how can one *not* like it?—but it means she has no notion of how holographic simulation underlies the concept.

At the board, I chalk a church spire for them, and trace it through aspiration, inspiration, respiration, perspiration. "A 'library' isn't a word pulled out of someone's ass," I say, and show them the *libro* inside it, and the way that open reading leads us to "liberty." "Even 'language' itself": I circle the *lang*—the tongue—and then put "cunnilingus" on the board. Most of us— me too, I insist—survive a day cane-tapping our way through structures we don't see.

That's what Bill Bryson claims: "I was on a long flight across the Pacific . . . when it occurred to me . . . that I didn't know the first thing about the only planet I was ever going to live on. I had no idea, for example, why the oceans were salty but the Great Lakes weren't. . . . I didn't know what a proton was, or a protein, didn't know a quark from a quasar." (Add to that, I'm willing to bet, what kept the plane invisibly held in the air.) And so he writes his marvelous info-larded best-selling *A Short History of Nearly Everything.* Facts, facts, facts. Except, because he's honest, it's also a history of what we still *don't* comprehend—an annals of absence.

This is even more startling his next time around: *At Home* is a room-by-room history of the house in which he lives. Compare that compact span to the open-bordered aura of *Nearly Everything!* And even so, the facts, facts, facts, and their knockable doors and tiles and joists and balustrades, are all-over pocked like Swiss cheese with the empty holes of what we don't know: "How Aspdin invented his product has always been something of a mystery" (page 223); "Why AT&T engineers chose the youthful Dreyfuss for the project is forgotten" (231); "a shadowy figure named Charles Bridgeman. Where exactly this dashing man of genius came from has always been a mystery" (256); "the fashion became to make things look natural. Where this impulse came from isn't at all easy to say" (257); "Soon the woods of North America were so full of plant hunters that it is impossible to tell now who exactly discovered what" (265); "the whereabouts of the mortal remains of quite a number of worthies [then an on-rolling list] are today quite unknown" (271);

"The identity of the vine owner is now lost, which is unfortunate as he was a significant human being" (277); "Yet, strangely, [Jefferson] didn't keep a diary or an inventory of Monticello itself. 'We know more about Jefferson's house in Paris than this one, oddly enough,' Susan Stein, the senior curator, told me" (295); "in the United States . . . it is known that about twelve thousand people a year hit the ground and never get up again, but whether that is because they have fallen from a tree, a roof, or off the back porch is unknown" (307); "No one knows where stairs originated or when, even roughly" (312).

This, from fewer than 100 pages out of 452, and all of it bountiful with emptiness.

(Amazing: we know more about the origin of *stars* than of *stairs*.)

As for me, I've decided to pioneer an existence that's Internet-free. I've never touched a computer keyboard, not once. What follows—never sent or received an e-mail, shopped online or paid a bill there, no eBay, online porn, or social networking, not one Google moment, or Nook, or Kindle, not one Wikipedia glance—is a willful illiteracy; is a life that's increasingly anti-matter; a charcoal stag or a reindeer that's itself, that's *more* itself, because of everything it's not.

The flame feeds off the lump of fat, as the bull on the wall feeds on the darkness.

Yes—and when in-person or postal paying-of-bills is no longer an option?

Mr. Bison Man, Big Aurochs Man, in the boulder-closed cave, with his frozen ecstatic leap across the cosmos, with the little spears drawn in his body.

3.

It's common to suppose that a Luddite wants less. That's what refusal must mean. But in fact a Luddite wants more—of the same. If I had enough space I'd devote an entire room to the museumly care of early manual typewriters. As it is, my few mementos of that vanishing world are dear to me . . . and the blue mesh bag of typewriter keys that Peggy gave me is doubly dear. Their gibberish jumble evokes an earlier world, when they were ordered, in rows, and created rows of language; just as they also evoke an earlier world when energy was ordered into a living system we all called "Peggy Rabb."

She'd meet me for noshes or drinks and beautiful boisterous poetry gab. "No need to wander as lonely as a cloud today," she'd say, and in a while there we'd be, talking the Lake District poets over cheese grits.

Now that diner is also gone.

It's tough for my undergraduate students to think of Wordsworth as edgy and rebellious; he's too fuddy-duddy rhythmic and seemingly prissy to their ears. But when I teach his sonnet "The World Is Too Much with Us" I always emphasize its radical— even dangerous—last lines. I say, "Just think about it. His is a far more uniformly (and uniformly policed) religious universe. He's grown up with stories of people who were pilloried for criticizing the church. And here he's outright saying that if it would only help him see the world again in its natural cycles, free of artificial factory time and market economy, he'd forsake his Christianity and return to the faith of an ancient religion. *I'd rather be / A pagan suckled in a creed outworn . . . / Have sight of Proteus rising from the sea; / Or hear old Triton blow his wreathèd horn.* I mean—wow!

In his essay "Prehistoric Eyes," Guy Davenport offers a similar wish, toward a similar reinvigorating . . . but Davenport's retroencompass is millennia-long in a way that makes the briny Greek sea-gods seem contemporary: "I would swap eyes, were it possible, with an Aurignacian hunter; I suspect his of being sharper, better in every sense."

He's been contemplating the cave wall art and the bones that bear engraved lines, like the Sarlat bone—the rib of an ox—that was marked up with a flint burin 230,000 years ago. His mind is inquisitive and empathetic and laser-point sharp, and he's read the scholars whose lifework is communing with these artifacts—he refers to "Alexander Marshack's brilliant speculative study of prehistoric symbolism"—but still, he knows we ultimately bump against unknowingness: "the images on the Sarlat bone . . . mean nothing to our eyes." They may be a "work of art, or plat of hunting rights, tax receipt, star map, or whatever," but finally all we have to hold are "gratuitous assumptions about the creature we call Cave Man." The bone is scored with seventy lines, and they tease us with radiant, gut-wrench, heart-exalting meaningfulness, the way a fifth dimension might—but entrance is denied us. "For this . . . ," as Wordsworth tells us in his sonnet, "we are out of tune."

The reindeer's antlers rise up like the elegantly fractaled map of a riverine system. The bulls mate. Or they fight. Or they're superimposed at random. At best we can guess, and our guesses are balsa-wood flecks on a turbulent sea of darkness. Once we were certain that the small rolled scrolls of clay that we've found in a scatter on some of the cave floors were the penis sheaths of adolescent males brought to the innermost sanctums for ritual initiation—or, anyway, symbols of phalluses. Now we think they were merely tests, scrolled up to see if the clay was of viable pliability, then discarded. Davenport: "Context has been the great problem of understanding [these images]. Breuil, a priest, tended to see them as religious; Leroi-Gourhan posited a sexual context. . . . Marshack places them in time, in the seasons, and relates them to the hunt." Impressive guesses, all. And when we're finished bringing ourselves to these animals, there they still are, more than impressive, moving us in exactly the way they should: outside of history. Thurman quotes one scholar: "The more you look, the less you understand."

We can't find the words. We can't get back to whatever words are appropriate: these animals are like the dreams we had in the womb. See?—"like." It's the best we can do. They bypass all of our articulation, powerful exactly because their presence doesn't require it. Their strength is that they *aren't* any vocabulary we can provide, or any of our vocabulary's referents. As I said, today I'm thinking, hard, about absence.

In his daffodils poem, "I Wandered Lonely as a Cloud," Wordsworth is healed of psychic distress by remembering an encounter, a joyful encounter, with those flowers. But he needs to remember "in vacant . . . mood"—he needs a blankness. Only then, in *that* space, can the daffodils "flash upon that inward eye."

This is the matrix, the nothingdark, the Mystery, that enables the horse to emerge like a cloud of muscle from its otherworld life, and the bulls to charge across a frieze that isn't a frieze so much as it is an open-ended possibility-field, and the does to prance (or thunder) (or cavort) from a rend in the rock face that might be (or not) the first creation-vent in time, from which the creatures of Earth streamed forth in their fruitfulness, "two by two," as we would learn to say in our own small way, so many millennia later.

I was the one who dropped off Peggy Rabb at Wesley Memorial Hospital, up on Hillside. It was no big deal, she said. It was stomach distress and constipation, and she'd get it checked out, but it was no big deal. She didn't bring an overnight bag. She didn't require a book or a magazine. And so I left her at the check-in counter. She turned around and smiled that great engaging veldt of a smile of hers, and waved, palm out, her fingers extended, something like a star a child would draw. Good-bye, she waved to me.

There aren't many *entire* human figures in the caves. But there are the handprints—so evocative! Most of them were formed by placing the hand flat on the cave wall and blowing—through a tube—a careful aerosol of paint around it. That is, they're negative images. Herzog ends his film about the caves with a long and steady shot of one of them, a shape in a mist of nearly un-imaginably archaic red, burning into our memories.

The hand is here because it isn't.

Wuramon

On the scale of ancient communities, it's a line of rubble, layers deep in the earth, that—from a distance, as we look at the fresh cross-sectioned side of the archaeological shaft—seems over millennia to have been compacted down to an even thinness, a horizontal quarter mile of pencil line. A few feet above it runs another one. A few feet lower, another.

These are a calendar—of hundreds of years. Each represents the absolute demolishment of a Neolithic village: all of its buildings—stone, mud-brick—staved in and leveled and then used as a base on which the village would be rebuilt. (At Çatalhöyük we've discovered eighteen levels of successive habitation.) For them this was easier than *repairing* the homes, the garrison, the temple; simply, they started over. And simply, we can use these wafery demarcations as metric devices sequencing the ends and reascensions of a single location of human living, over generations.

Yes, and on the scale of *one* life . . . ? That would come to what the bioarchaeologists call "Beau's lines," fine striations that develop when a fingernail stops growing (say, due to disease) and then begins again . . . ends and reascensions. On the only fingernail left attached to that body the Otztal Alpine glaciers had preserved from about 5,300 years ago—"the Iceman," as we've nicknamed that astonishingly intact cadaver, no more out of its true shape than the freeze-dried plum in an astronaut's pouch—are the telltale signs that he had confronted serious illness three times in the months before he dragged himself off to die (from an arrow injury) into a shallow, rocky mountain pass. They look like tiny stress lines on a sherd of scrimshaw ivory.

And on the scale of meteorology, it's wind—it's globally ambient crosscurrents of wind; it's strands of olive boughs that act as voice box for the lengthy, haunting kyrie of the wind, with full laryngeal and pulmonary force; it's the airborne continent's-worth of soil that circles the planet as grit in the grip of the wind; it's the pollenologist's study of how far wind disburses the sexual seeking of plant for plant, of fluctuation in cereal resources and in climate. Yes, and on the scale of one life, it's the pollen from a small tree called "hop hornbeam," lodged in the food residue of an Iron Age colon: somebody abrim with love-itch and despairs as complaining as yours or mine . . . has died, we can determine now, in the late spring or the early summer, the time of hop hornbeam's flowering.

"Economics," we say—abstract and gassy. Of course it's also a woman, actual, heavy, hair unrooted and drifting away from her scalp from hunger, here in a daub-and-wattle hut on an otherwise clement day in 1828 in an upland valley. If we were there, we could smell the sourness flimmering off her skin.

Or "musicology," we say, which is an admirable field of theory. We can't forget, however, that it blends without caesura into the body of someone so long-term devoted to her cello that the two become a symbiotic unit. Her body is mainly the space in which a cello comes alive, singing inside her spraddle.

On the scale of ho-hum homily, it's "Be careful what you wish for: you might get it." On the scale of an individual life, it's molten gold a concentrating Aztec warrior pours, a cupful, down the throat of a captive—one of Cortés's men.

It's always that way, as in the word "interface": its first two general syllables, and then the specific body part.

The intellectualized, no matter how airily indeterminate, is never completely severed from its correlative in flesh and bone. "Intellectualized"—and where does *that* happen, if not in the gnarled, link-marbled meat of the brain? The strife of *The Iliad* is measurable in anybody's chest, in cardiovascular heaves. The high declamations of *Romeo and Juliet* are repeated every day, by salt, by protein, in the miles of whispering gallery in the groin.

And the "soul"? Is there a physical counterpart to the soul? I don't know. But you can see, at least, the physical vessel of its journeying, on display here in a hall in my university, part of "one of the largest and most important collections of Asmat art in existence . . . over 950 works." The Asmat—from "an inhospitable environment" says the placard, in western New Guinea. There are shields, house poles, ancestor figures, and as I've said, this "soul ship" far removed now from its original travel, and overlooking the various pale, underpaid scholars and sleepy, distracted undergraduate students of Wichita State . . . this ship that was fashioned to voyage into the realm of the spirits.

And we can't hold a thought in our hands the way we can a pear, a breast; but we can knock against the skull in which the thought once bloomed, at least. Ask Hamlet.

We can't weigh the leap of love we ascribe to the heart; but we could search for Yorick's sternum in the dirt. There are symbols—residences, even—of the invisible, things with obvious poundage and nap.

The "soul" . . . at least we can see the grain of its wooden shell, here, on this wall now, as the side of the ship is revealed in the late Kansas afternoon light.

Who *was* it?—that's right: Jim, who else helped organize (or anyway, helped organize with such panache and unfrayed affability) the trip of all the members of the American Museum of Asmat Art in St. Paul, Minnesota, to Wichita State, in Kansas, for the opening night ("the gala," as the PR said) of the Holmes Museum of Anthropology's *Spirit Journeys* exhibit of Asmat cult goods? Oh, it was Jim all right, Jim Czarniecki (say ZAHR-nicki), the go-to guy, the unflappable, the generosity engine. Jim the radiant. Jim with the face of a full-force lighthouse lens that alchemized whatever was the object of its gaze to a golden occasion.

Jim the connoisseur: of art: of wine: of the very bricks in a gallery's walls or a restaurant's gate, and what an amazing fin de siècle harborfront cathedral they originally constructed in the days before their un- (and then re-) doing here, in this very place we were visiting, yes right now, with him and Anne, because he knew of it and he knew that we'd enjoy it, whatever gallery-or-restaurant-of-the-moment it was, and we needed, we *needed,* to be swept up in his dynamo whooshes and brought here for an evening's epic anecdotes, for badinage as intricately strategized as championship chess and yet as weightlessly spun as floss. *That* Jim.

It certainly wasn't required that I like him. He was only the baggage that came along with his wife, my editor, Anne, when Skyler and I flew out to an awards ceremony in LA. But I liked him. Skyler liked him. He was solemn when appropriate—he listened, with the rumpled-forehead semiotic of "strict attention." He was the raconteur when it was time to have a raconteur. He doted on Anne. (How often does anybody "dote" these days? The world is sore in need of doteship.) Of that loud, chaotic blah-blah night of fake-grin-handshake crowded rooms and too, too many new names to remember, and dead-end streets, he made a tame and manageable thing—the way the good mahout on the elephant does, so you hardly notice: only a subtle pressure of the knees. He told his story about the opening of the Pollock show, when a dog trots in, and . . . *rrring,* "Excuse me a minute," his cell phone; back in Minneapolis somebody needs a circus tent the next day for a charity raffle—*a circus tent.* "Just give me a moment." He leaves, he's back. "So a dog trots in, with paint all over its paws . . ."—he's got them their circus tent. Jim Czarniecki, a new energy source, a runaway sun, a maverick sizzle escaped from the heart of an element of roiling potential. Jimonium. The man was inexhaustible.

A miscellany: The photo of Anne and Jim and the kids on vacation with his relatives in Montana: spurts of rapids water, eggy white and sunshot, clamor around the raft as thickly as a covey of doves. The photo of monumental ice sculptures, some of them Babylonian in authority and elegance. The story of when the mayor's errant golf ball brained a browsing cow: and so now there's a charity golf day (always a charity, always a two-fisted largehearted cause) with a culminating contest: teeing off and knocking over a plywood cow. Jim thaumaturgically simmering with inventive goodwill. The photos from Spain. The photo of Anne and Jim below a soul ship on the museum wall in Wichita.

I revisited it, the week after the gala. And now, alone with it in that hall, I found its otherworldly presence even more . . . *something;* magisterial? spooky? "Otherwordly," I said, and yet the soul ship—*wuramon,* in the Asmat—can be up to forty feet long; and a forty-foot-length of wood is hardly spectral. A dugout canoe capacious enough for twenty carved occupants, plus decoration of feathers, seeds, and leaves, is hardly phantasmal: in one photograph, it requires fourteen men for its lifting.

These are the various occupants of a *wuramon: etsjo* (or *eco*), human-like figures, always crouched facedown, and always with penises that, as Tobias Schneebaum's *Asmat Images* puts it, are "horizontal, anti-gravity"; the *ambirak,* a being that lives at the bottom of rivers and streams; *okom,* a spirit "shaped like a Z," that crawls along the same watery silt-floors as the *ambirak; mbu,* the turtle, symbol of fertility (by virtue of its copious eggs); *jenitsjowotsz,* a female spirit, always facing forward; and "usually included, as well, are the hornbill head, *jirmbi;* the black king cockatoo head, *ufirmbi;* a decapitated head, *kawe;* and a *was* design, representing either a cuscus tail or an open space in the jungle." Every figure has a different carver, all of them under the expert supervision of a "maestro carver." An object like that can't help but have a weighty, declarative character; it can't help but remind us it was once the trunk of the *os eyok* tree, rooted firmly, greedily, into the earth.

But I said *other*-worldly, and otherworldly it surely is—this vessel with its wooden reenactments of life-forms almost like—and yet not like—our own. In part, the wonder-evoking, supernatural aspect of the *wuramon* is because it's never created with a bottom to it. That's right, it has no bottom to it: "the spirits have no need of one." As if they're flaunting their supraskills. As if they're beyond such a mundane consideration as navagability.

Completely open to the water, it still doesn't sink; in fact, if anything, it appears to arrow assuredly through water and air on its mysterious business with a mastery no earthly ship could ever hope to achieve. As if an invisible layer of spirit world one micron thick entirely and durably coats this ship and its inhabitants. And where they originate?—I don't know. And where they're bound for?—I couldn't say. Ancestral *and* far-future simultaneously, they seem to be some unacknowledged part of us—the ghost part, maybe, the part where our clairvoyance and our eternal selves reside—and they're here in our daily domain as a strange reminder/encouragement of what awaits us, one day, when we waver on out of our bodies and join the spirits completely.

Interesting. And then, of course, I returned to the "daily domain"—returned to raking the razor tines of that year's income tax over the softening clay of my brain, returned to papers to grade, and votes to cast, and the trellis of marriage that always needs to be repaired and sometimes merely asks to have its overscribble of vines and flowers appreciated.

One day the car gives up; I hear the clash of its tectonic plates, the shrill of its electron bondings separating. One day I hear a colleague sob behind her office door, like a captive people behind an iron wall. One day: *achoo!* One day: oh boy! One day the high hilarity is a student paper that says, quote, *This is a poet who copulates words and meaning together.* One day I buy a new car, or really it's a month of many days, because the experience is so slimy, I can only do it in tiny, tentative units. One day the war. One day the celebrity news. One day: stampeding sasquatches of emotion. One day: a total snooze. One day a phone call: he only had cramps; but it wouldn't stop; they had to remove a blockage from his colon, and it was malignant; it had metastasized, they found out, to his liver, and maybe a lymph node, maybe it rode around like a satellite in his circulatory system now; they didn't know yet how bad it was, but in any case "it doesn't look good." Jim. *No.* Oh yes: Jim Czarniecki.

It begins with the men going into the jungle, and then to a special encampment there, drumming and singing all night. In the morning, the tree—a huge *os eyok*—is uprooted. The tree is carefully chosen: the tree will become a *wuramon*. Its branches are removed; the trunk is painted, red, white, black; fresh fruit from along the river is hung upon it; and then, with sober purpose and yet much merriment, it's carried back to the village and planted upside down in front of the men's cult house: and there it waits for the *emak tsjem,* the "bone house"—the male initiates' house—to be built.

The bone house must be completed in one day—this is tradition with the force of law. And once it's done, the initiates of that season (their faces painted with soot now) enter it and remain inside it until the *wuramon* is ready.

Weeks pass. Everybody waits until the sago worms are mature and distributed. These are the fat tree worms of the area—the larvae of the Capricorn snout beetle—that, whether roasted or alive, are such an important delicacy at Asmat feasts. Sometimes they can be studiously chewed, in sacred ritual; at others, fisted up casually like popcorn. In their living state, they look like giant, writhing thumbs; they look like glistening nuggets of elephant tusk come damply to life. And when the sago worms are distributed, then—and only then—does the carving begin.

When the soul ship is finished, it's painted (the same red, white, black colors) and decorated. Women are admitted into the men's cult house (the only occasion on which this happens), and they uncover the newly completed *wuramon*. After ritual food exchange (the *emak cen pakmu,* the "bone house feast"), the *wuramon* is lifted onto the shoulders of its carvers and, to a background of drumming, chanting, and bamboo horns, it's carried over to the bone house and placed on the front porch, under a carved-wood crocodile head, *ee karoan,* a spirit who fills the initiates with bravery.

In fact, the whole of the bone house is constructed to imbue the sequestered initiates with the qualities of ideal manhood: *wukai* gives them wisdom, as does the *sawar* fish (to whom they touch their foreheads), the *tem as* figure imparts fertility, the *jirai* fish instills in them "the light of goodness," etc. Over all of the weeks of waiting there, these qualities have entered them, patiently, unceasingly, seeping in a little a day, smelting them, refocusing them—and now, at last, they enter the world: a second birth: into manhood.

As a final ritual gesture, they slide, one at a time, across the soul ship's *mbu* (or sometimes *okom*) figure—and then each one "is scarified across his chest with a mussel shell." The next day, the chests of initiate girls are similarly scarified. "And after all have been scarified, they return to their own homes, and sleep."

This isn't a summer afternoon in Columbus, Ohio, or Jackson, Mississippi, or Springfield, Illinois. A weirdly exotic beauty (for us), a potent repulsion (for us), a vigorously primal spirituality (for us)—these braid their way through the Asmat ceremony; these assault our sense of the everyday. It isn't washing your car in the driveway. It isn't screaming for the hometown Fighting Cobras to clobber the visiting Wild Bulls.

And yet . . . "During 'rest days,' following 'labor days,' they will often cleanse—in a manner that can only be thought of as 'ritualized'—their travel-machines. A bucket is used, inside of which a certain proportion of 'cleanser-liquid' is added to the water." Or: "The ceremonial rivalry of 'teams' on the field is matched in the articulation of socially-sanctioned frenzy by the clamorous rites of those in attendance ('in the stands') and by the nubile muses of this event, who posture gymnastically in between its ongoing phases." It's all one, I suspect, to the anthropologists spying upon our species from their extragalactic observatories. (For *us;* for them, they aren't "extra-" anything; they're comfy in the one and only galaxy that matters.)

If it's "odd" to us, this picture of an Asmat man who sleeps on the skull an ancestor for a pillow . . . that unnerving almost-symmetry . . . well, I've met Charlie, who once earned his living in one of New York's tonier artiste-and-love-nest districts by fashioning glitzorama custom-designed armoires and fainting couches for a hip upscale clientele (Yoko Ono was one of his clients), the hook of his product being that every inch was upholstered in vibrant snakeskin. (I don't know his business's name—if it ever had one—but Up Scale would have been clever.) It's all the same, I suspect, to the scanner eyes of the scholars from Galaxy X.

Oh? Even (and here I quote from photograph captions in Schneebaum's account of his time among the Asmat) the man seen "cutting out a small window in a felled sago tree, into which this owner will put moss that has first been rubbed around his anus and armpits"? Even "the adoption ceremony, when newly adopted individuals crawl through a tunnel representing the birth canal, the ceiling of which is a row of the widespread legs of the new adoptive mothers"? Even "the bride being carried into the house of the groom by the mother's brother"?—this, with the injunction "Note the bride price (one stone axe) on her shoulder, and also the three pairs of boar tusks at her uncle's elbow that indicate he has taken three heads in battle."

Yes: even then; even these. On the scale of deltas being accreted grain-of-silt by grain-of-silt, on the scale of meteor showers and of zephyrs, and on the Carl Sagan scale of those scientific students of the skies that I've ascribed to Planet Ooga-Booga up there somewhere . . . none of this is any more implausible than a day at the NASCAR track; or than the Mayday Gay Day Float Parade in the Village; or than the windbag garrulosity Olympics as the tenure committee pisses its many contrarian opinions into its multicontrarian winds. I mean—have you *seen* the tumult of Parrotheads at a Jimmy Buffet concert?—or sat in slack-jawed gogglement at the weasel words slinking out of the jaws in a session of Congress lately? It must all even out, must equal something designated "human," on the Ooga-Boogans' version of an institute's statistical charts.

This leveling of difference is the outer space translation of the encompass we find in Robert Boyle's observation, responding to some inequities of Parliament's in the seventeenth century: "It is strange that men should rather be quarrelling for a few trifling opinions, wherein they dissent, than to embrace one another for those many fundamental truths wherein they agree."

So if the Asmat appear to us to exist in two (or more) parallel concepts of "time"; if simultaneously they live in the land of work and of feast, of holding the infant up to a breast, of felling the tree, of filling the bamboo tubes with drinking water, *and* in the land of walking under, over, and through the "middle world," *ndami ow,* that space between the living and the infinity realm of the spirits . . . we lead equally time-muddled lives, yes? Here in Atlanta, Schenectady, San Antonio, Fire Island, Astoria, Aspen, Philadelphia, Missoula, Santa Fe, Moline.

For example: at the Asmat exhibit, in maestro mode and leading us from shield to headband to ancestor pole, and greeting old friends with his great atomic reactor beams of enthusiasm, Jim Czarniecki was already—although we couldn't have known it—a host to the initial thickened cells that would betray him, that would start to bear him into an alternate future. At the champagne toasts in the restaurant in St. Paul, as we joked about the South Beach diet, and dissected the Democrats' strategy in that city: already, inside him, the cancer was starting to gauge its speed, its rampancy. We couldn't tell time by already-o'-clock, but its hands moved duly anyway. "Already": I've come to despise that word, and its breeding of secret tomorrows in the lining of our flesh.

And in Naperville, in Sarasota, in Taos, in Peoria—do we

possess a correlative to the complicated mazes of Asmat spirits? "Daily life is filled with spirits of the forest, spirits of the seas and rivers, spirits of the day and spirits of the night, as well as the spirits of ancestors of the distant past and those of the most recently dead." The most demanding spirits?—"those who had been decapitated, their anger eventually forcing the men of their village to avenge their deaths."

When a person sleeps, his or her *ndamup* is able to flow from the body—a "shadow" or "image"—and roam around; it can metamorphose into other forms of life, like a crocodile. In addition to that, every villager is endowed with a *ndet* (and given an *ndet* name) several months, or even more than a year, after birth (for the *ndet* is too powerful a force to be housed in the very young: it completes that person's individual character). All living things have their *ndet*, even a tree or a tuft of grass, and so do certain inanimate objects: statues, prowheads, ceremonial poles. There is also *yuwus*. There is also *samu*. "Spirit children enter human bodies and animate embryos."

Some spirits are courted and honored. The apotheosis of this must be the twenty-foot-tall ancestor pole, so phallic in its up-thrust shape. Schneebaum says, "Human figures and birds, painted red and white and black, are carved on it one above the other. It is a powerful affirmation of virility and fertility, as if all the male spirits of the carving have combined and are about to explode and ejaculate their life force onto all below." Other, evil spirits must be guarded against, and Schneebaum witnesses women who come across a corpse and immediately fling off their skirts, and then throw themselves naked into the mud, to roll around—to hide the smells of their bodies from any predator spirits skulking about. One comes to believe that if they acquire vocabulary like "molecule," "neutrino," "synapse," "megahertz" . . . the Asmat will quickly invent a set of spirits to surround these, too—to plague them, or exalt them.

Here in Tucson and Topeka and Eugene . . . the collateral branches of this family of thought are going strong, and always have been. Here, as evidence: John Aubrey, in his forthright seventeenth-century prose: "When Dr Powell preacht, a Smoake would issue out of his head; so great agitation of Spirit he had." Or sudden table-rap and trumpet-blat at a nineteenth-century séance, with an ectoplasmic coil as thick as a hawser rope at the side of the medium's head where it rests in her crossed arms, and a hollow voice of imprecation and sweet, platitudinous comfort from the Other Side. The Ooga-Booga dissertation candidates say *what* about the wine the priest transmogrifies to holy blood, about the little buzz-saw whirl of dybbuks that tormented the Prophet's followers in the desert wastes, about the rabbi's absolute assurance that an access lane exits between his kasha-scented murmurs and the all-receptive Ear of the Creator? Here in Phoenix, here in Akron, here in Laramie.

"If personality exists after what we call death, it is reasonable to conclude that those who leave this Earth would like to communicate with those they have left here." BIG "if," I say; but who am I to argue against the Asmat—or, in this case, Thomas Edison, who went on to write, "I am inclined to believe that our personality hereafter will be able to affect matter. If this reasoning be correct, then, if we can evolve an instrument so delicate as to be affected or moved and manipulated by our personality as it survives in the next life, such an instrument, when made available, ought to record something."

Working the same assumptions, a group that called itself the Spirit Electronic Communication Society, of Manchester, England, was formed in 1949. Their founder—a Dutchman, a Mr. N. Zwaan—the year before at a meeting of the International Spiritualism Federation, had demonstrated "an electronic device which produced a field of energy capable of stimulating the psychic senses into activity"—the "Super-ray," he called it, then the "Zwaan ray," and this developed into the "Teledyne," then the "Telewave." The claim for these?—"a form of direct communication, by voice, with the dead."

To this day, there remains a small but serious and dedicated circle of electro-perceptual researchers who are sure they can manifest—through everything from enormous sparkling coil-and-pylon-studded machines, to the everyday background static of a cell phone—the otherwise unheard (although ubiquitous) speech of Those Beyond: the discarnate.

"They have," says Tina Laurant, "their own peculiar rhythm and pitch. However, I do, on playback, always listen with the speed slowed down, [and this way] high-pitched noises or sounds will be turned into intelligible speech." These utterances, it would seem, abound as bountifully, as astonishingly, in the air as do (when our eyes are attuned) the wingèd green-faced goats and friendly, levitating cows and anemone-colored angels of Marc Chagall.

One photograph in a book I own: a Hasidic Jew at the Wailing Wall in Jerusalem, in his centuries-old style of black religious wear, is holding a mobile phone against the stone . . . and the voice of a relative hundreds of miles away intones the ancient prayers.

The woman becomes increasingly lovely as she becomes increasingly clear—the line of her, below the fussing dust brush of an archaeology lab assistant working on those limestone flakes that served as scrap for personal jottings and doodles among the artisans who labored on tombs in the Valley of the Kings around 1300 BC. (These small and quotidian glimpses into their lives—love poems, sly caricatures of overseers, etc.—have managed to triumph over the forces of time's erasure with a success that's often *not* matched by the sanctioned, careful inscriptions on the tomb walls, which the pharaohs of ancient Egypt assumed would last as long as the sand itself, and would guarantee their own resplendent welcome into the afterlife.)

There's a necessarily sexual component to her profile. After all, she's naked, crouched low with a corresponding uplift to her haunches and ass, and the text to the left explains that we find her "blowing into the oven": her lips are pursed around a tube about a forefinger long. She's young and ripe. To not see the eroticism here would be, I think, to need to admit to one's own incompletion. Even so, the casual domesticity of the scene is, at the same time, miles away from the erotic. It might say "drudgery" to a contemporary of hers, or "familial nourishment." It could be that this aspect of the sketch—the kitchen ambience— serves partially as a pretext for erotic display, the way it appears to do so in the guileless poses of dewy, toiling laundresses and dancers in Degas's work. On the other hand, the demands of baking as pictured here—again, for a contemporary of hers— might well have folded the erotic almost unrecognizably into the bulk of a larger concern, like a yolk folded into dough.

What's clear in any case is the eloquence of this simple line of brown ink: as it rounds her thighs and butt cheeks, and then arches about to become the vigorous hunch of her back—as it makes shaped space from nothingness—it becomes as fully articulate as the architect's svelte line that creates the dome of a mosque or the rounded roof over a stadium. So delicate!—and so authorial in expression. On the scale of professional fulfillment, it must be extraordinary, watching as the scrupulous application of wash and the finicky swish of the dust brush bring this figure slowly out of the concealing darks of fifteen hundred years, one thin gradation of further lucidity at a time.

But on the scale of me, this idea comes down to watching my wife asleep, as night begins to thin from an obdurate black opacity to a slightly more permissive shade of char . . . and there she is, like the shape of a fossil just starting to show itself from the hold of a nugget of coal.

It always works that way: a spectrum with the Big Stuff at its one end—Evolution; Ethics; Art—and at its other end, the hard and spot-on details of an "I." No matter how far apart, they partake of a shared continuum.

On the level of theories of temperament, it's the ancient world's conception of phlegm, blood, yellow bile, and black bile that gets passed along to the Middle Ages and Renaissance as "the four humors"—each of those liquid substances responsible for one of four aspects of mental and bodily being. "Health is dependent on the final equilibrium of these elements, while an excess of any one produces disease." Too much black bile produces melancholy. Saturn is the melancholic's planet ("sinister, brooding, secluded Saturn"), and it works, along a complicated scientifico-mystical grid of connections, in conspiracy with the rise of that tarry fluid in the body's own deep wells.

That's as compelling as our own late twentieth-century grids of connective systems: "Scientists have repeatedly found brain pathology when conducting imaging studies (pictures taken of the brain, such as positron-emission tomography scans) of the anatomy and functioning of the brains of patients with depression, schizophrenia, or manic-depression—showing, for example, in bipolar patients that there is an enlargement of the amygdala;

an increase in white-matter lesions, known as hyperintensities, which are associated with the water content of brain tissue; and severe depletions in the number of glial cells." To every era, its own selected avenues of linguistic approach to the blues.

But all of this notwithstanding on the level of my friend Dana, it's a sexual spate of mania one night in 1989 of such extreme proportion, it involved—by the time the sun first lit the various grimes of a squad house on the Near North Side of Chicago—a visiting rugby team, ten magnums of cheap champagne, the contents of the broken-into costume trunk at a school for circus clowns, a three-car pileup, four cop cars, and (not least of these ingredients) Dana's mother on her knees in front of a potbellied chief of detectives, with those tears on her face of the kind that encourage the gods of ancient Greek tragedy— the gods of cannibalism and human sacrifice and incest—to consider coming out of their long retirement for the screams of this moment.

That's how it *is*. On the level of the biosphere, it's "interaction among ecological niches." On a crazy day in November, however, somewhere in a creek near Baton Rouge, Louisiana, it's a $70,000 haul from the Lucky Dollar Casino the thieves had dumped out in the wilderness and an enterprising band of beavers had woven into the sticks and brush of their dam. Or the day in St. Cloud, Minnesota, in April 1985, when "several dozen starfish" rained inexplicably down "on the roofs and the yards of that city": starfish: *Minnesota*.

On the level of meteorology, it's a tsunami. On the level of desperation and of perfect-for-the-media secular miracle, it's Rizal Shahputra, swept off into what should have been the fatal waters—this, while holding on to the nine-year-old twins a neighbor had handed her—but she and the girls first "rested on a snake . . . as long as a telephone pole" (so says the *Jakarta Post;* the *Melbourne Herald Sun* reports, with less pizzazz, that instead they "followed in its wake") and survived on the makeshift raft the waters made a gift to her, in the form of an uprooted palm tree.

Here's another one. I step back, and it's centuries of book design: a dazzlingly curated show on the inventive engineering of pop-up (and similar "paper animation") books at the downtown Los Angeles Public Library gallery. Especially bright and impressive are those eighteenth-century books that telescope outward—colorful paper accordions—and when you look through one end's offered peephole, it's like staring down the megalength of a garden's flowery corridor or the successive rooms of Santa Claus's workshop, or the receding coral'd grottoes of an underwater city.

Skyler and I are there with Anne and Jim. It's one of the last of the trips on which we'll see him in his effusive glory, imbibing the life of every showcase, "Here! Look at this!"—his florid face at a pane of glass like a child's at a confectioner's window. Learnèd. Insouciant. *Now* of course it's all about the chemo, all about such words as "expectancy" and "colorectal." He said on the phone, "If it turns out for the best, I'll have a chronic disease that's still manageable," and the tone of his voice—this is Jim, after all—could have led you to think he was predicting chorus girls, a ticker-tape parade, a shower of Gummi Bears.

The alloys of his body are breaking the contract that they signed at birth, the microscopic Benedict Arnold cells of him are welcoming the opportunist enemy into their heartland, every part of him is open to physiological identity theft . . . and here he was, preparing for the flooding acid burn that we call medical containment, speaking genuinely to me of hope. Is any novel's hero more quixotic?

I look through a peephole in my side of that afternoon's telephone call, down the hallway of rooms in the time that I've known him, and somewhere in there is the pop-up show: "Check this one out! A mermaid and a waterfall!" Those centuries of book design arrive at that five-minute phone conversation: just the way an überword—"nobility," "injustice," "fortitude," "lust," "sangfroid," whatever—is finally only a temperature we understand by the way our skin responds.

To comprehend the American Revolution, we need to know the history of "natural rights philosophy," and the principles of British constitutionalism, as well as the abstract ideas of Rousseau, of Locke, and other Continental progressive thinkers. Then again, Thomas Jefferson said that to know the truest state of society's enlightenment, one "must ferret the people out of their hovels, . . . look into their kettle, eat their bread, loll on their beds." And surely both approaches have their place (and share their deepest substance) in a circling totality-calculus. Surely when we drill down to the marrow of "bed," the hemoglobin of "bed," and to the bottomrock of "kettle," and out the other side . . . we enter a salon where the philosophers are arguing political theory all night long, in vast and cloudy expatiating.

The Tweedledumesque of a general law is linked—although it may be over centuries of us, and over continents—to its twin, the Tweedledeeitude of one life's immediate urgencies. The arrow travels in both directions: T. S. Eliot, writing in "Tradition and the Individual Talent," says that new art must be judged inside the standards set by the art of the past— as the art of the past must be rethought in terms of the art of the moment. For some given example, it may look like a tenuous connection— but it's as certain as the mixoplasm marriage of human and animal in the creatures on the island of Dr. Moreau as they shamble, shoat-and-woman, ox-and-man, about the leafy shade-and-sunlight hills of their insular hideaway.

I remember once seeing a Sunday painter at work. He had set up his easel just outside a grove of oak, with his back to that shadowiness, and instead was squinting across a meadow, into the sunset, to capture its color (about the brandied-orange of a monarch's wings) in paint. His concentration was enormous. A little less rouge ... a little more umber ... ? At the same time, however, his artist's smock—his face, in fact, and the two small incandescent pools of his glasses—were a ready, susceptible canvas on which the sunset painted itself. A line from Randall Jarrell's poem "Field and Forest": "The trees can't tell the two of them apart."

On the level of the "literary essay," that's what I'm writing about—that two-way permeability. Every one of us: a thriving hive of -ology and -ism. But it won't mean a thing if it isn't manifested in our dreams and in our metabolic rumble.

We can talk all day about the sigmoidoscopy, about the heat of the IV drip and its resultant weakness, we can think of the length of intestine they—the masked and grandly remunerated "they"—clipped out, and we can bandy the clinicalese of that world with a frightening ease: "remission possibility," "squamous carcinoma," "Nigro radiation," "oncology protocol." It can't be avoided. It's "real." It's a part of instructional CD-ROMs and pamphlets.

Yes, but what I also think is this: the *wuramon* in Jim has slipped its moorings and entered the river of its voyaging a little in advance of the soul ships the rest of us have. He was always an adventurer.

It's bottomless, as they all are. It will either sink or float, will either be part of one world or another. In New Guinea, they gather at night on the dark woods-heavy shores, and they look at the wrinkled moonlight on the water's surface, and tell their ancient (and never outdated) tales of spirit pilgrimage.

On the scale of Jim Czarniecki, we're grouped along his circulatory current. The *wuramon* enters that flow. We love him, and we're waving.

Two Characters in Search of an Essay

1. JK

He was always the smallest, in any room, "an Atom of a man," somebody said (the word existed then, although not in our later sense); but spunky, quick to rise to a righteous indignation and to support it with a whirligig of fists.

"Terrier courage," one of his schoolfellows called it. In 1819 he was discovered brawling in the rich north London back-alley muck with a musclehead butcher's apprentice, who was "something of a bruiser" compared to Keats's own just-barely-topping-five-feet. This brutish opponent had been torment-ing a kitten. Keats won. Another early schoolfellow recalled that as a child, Keats was "not attached to books [but] he would fight any one—morning, noon, and night. The daring of his charac-ter, this pugnacity & generosity of disposition—in passions of tears or outrageous fits of laughter—always in extremes—made an impression on me." (A bit later on, after one impetuously youthful foray into a brothel, his chosen inamorata reported, "Proportionally, all of his Parts are in keeping with the General Heighth, but I must say his enthusiastic Persistence is nonpareil.")

"Today," the schoolmaster shouted out to his zoo of young charges, "we are going to be, each with a named role to play, the sun and its planets." This was at John Clarke's Enfield boarding school, and Keats was nine. (John Clarke was known as a liberal dissenter, and his headmaster skills were inventive. Thus, his attempt at an anthro-solar system.)

He pointed. "Bunt Watkins, please position yourself in the center, here, unmovingly." Bunt Watkins was the stoutest; he was commonly called Barrel Bunt. "You, Master Watkins, by the privilege of your imposing rotundity, shall be our Sun."

And then the rest of the sky was assigned. Seven students: seven planets; and a few unruly comets and meteors sent to gallop through at an angle. It made for exuberant pandemonium, though not chaos exactly: all of this schoolyard energy was still in the interest (or so Clarke wishfully theorized) of demonstrating celestial organization.

"And if you please, Master Keats, our Mighty Minuscule, do us the honor to run way back . . . no, farther on . . . yes, there . . . past the brook . . . and be a tiny distant pinprick of Starlight."

Clarke intended this as a left-handed honor: representing all of the rest of the Firmament. But needless to say there was laughter at this, not all of it genial. "Pinprick" was Keats's name for the remainder of the term.

So there he was, on his faraway own, a star; which is also a sun, irradiant, thermonuclear, perfect as a symbol for the passions and ambitions that roiled inside him and sought release. Although nobody pointed this out as he stood there, still and alone, while the planets enjoyed their afternoon recess of whooping orrery orbiting.

And eventually he would recognize the sun to be an image of his early infatuation with . . . what would the word be? . . . Art? Inspiration? Parnassus? . . . The sun, become a golden access lane to the realm of the Muse.

By 1815, however, he was well on the way—increasingly reluctantly—to a medical life, to become a Surgeon. Already he had risen from a "dresser" (the assistant to the practicing Surgeon) and then had obtained an apothecary's license, and now was enrolled for a completing course of instruction at Guy's Hospital. But beguiled by the ever-more-undeniable urge to become a Poet . . . not a dabbler, no, but a man of literary vivacities fully steeped from awaking to candle-snuff in the quest for poetic excellence, a Poet recognizably so in the very marrow! . . . he felt himself, more every day, as trapped inside his studies as an anatomical specimen is buried inside a resin brick.

Perhaps his closest confidant at the time was Charles Cowden Clarke—the son of Keats's old schoolmaster—who remembered that the drone of medical seminars would run "from him like water from a duck's back." When together they read Spenser's *Faerie Queen,* Keats "went through it as a young horse would through a spring meadow—ramping." But preparing the cannula to drain a wound? Reciting a list of nerves in the buttocks? Clarke remembered Keats telling him, "The other day, during the lecture, there came a sunbeam into the room, and with it a whole troop of creatures floating in the ray; and I was off with them to Oberon and Fairy-land."

Perhaps other Worlds are contiguous with our own! Perhaps there are Worlds in concentric circles! And when they touch, once in a century . . . ! He had an occasional vision of a man in a shaggy beast-skin robe—a priest-king? a healer? This figure was here on Earth for the space of one astonished breath, and then . . . gone! Perhaps . . .

". . . can observe the hemispherical bisymmetry. And the term for the removal of the brain from the cranium . . . ? Mister John Keats?" *[dazed silence]* "I say there, Mister Keats, you are to *answer* this question, not *enact* it."

He longed to be "among the English poets." The giants. The undying. "Many and many a verse I hope to write," he says in *Endymion*.

Charles Cowden Clarke was there at what's arguably the first of the legend-behind-the-masterpiece stories. Clarke had acquired a 1616 folio edition of George Chapman's verse translation of *The Iliad*. For Keats, as biographer Robert Mighall puts it, "poetry had replaced medicine as a demanding full-time discipline"—this time a discipline that quickened his blood. The two friends stayed up the night, until 6:00 a.m., drinking and reading aloud passages of that thick-packed, gloryful seventeenth-century language, their eyes lit with the campfires of an ancient savage pageantry, and their tongues apotheosized to something grander. Clarke said that Keats "sometimes shouted" with delight.

In the thinly lightening rag-end of the night, Keats made the two-mile walk from Clerkenwell, where Clarke lived, back to his student lodgings in Southwark, his head filled with "teeming wonderment," and his heart and his breaths and his steps like chips of balsa wood abob on an iambic pentameter chop.

It was dark. But the last of the moon still relayed a bank shot of sun . . . *And with it a whole troop of creatures floating in the ray.* It was dark, but his path was golden.

By 10:00 a.m. a clean copy of his sonnet "On First Looking into Chapman's Homer" was delivered to Clarke's breakfast table.

One senses that Keats's description of amazed exploration refers not only to his spirited introduction to Chapman, nor even to the poem's famous climactic moment, the discovery of the Pacific by Western eyes, but also to the night's unveiling of his own instantaneous powers.

> Then felt I like some watcher of the skies
> When a new planet swims into his ken

"Sweet are the pleasures that to verse belong," one early piece begins. But he saw, too, more and more, how—in addition to flights of inspired rhapsodizing—poetry's deepest pleasures required deep dedication, strategizing, refining. "I have asked myself so often why I should be a Poet more than other Men, seeing how great a thing it is,—how great things are to be gained by it." Mighall says his goal now was "to measure up to the august ideals he had set for his art."

A neighbor once called Keats "quite the little Poet." Keats riposted: that was like calling Napoleon "quite the little Soldier."

It was dark, but his path was golden.

2. CT

Luckily for him, there are tornadoes in Kansas.

Yes; they'll pick up a man or a woman like a cork doll, and they'll flatten a house, a barn, as if it's a cardboard box for matches. In the aftermath, the hairs from a horse's tail have been discovered driven through wood. Anybody who lives in Burdett, Kansas, knows this. Anybody who spends one sweaty minute in its wheat fields, there with nothing but sky 360 degrees around, just sky and endless vulnerability, knows this. It's smart to have a tornado cellar somewhere close that a family can run to when a hundred roaring dinosaurs of wind roll out of the sick-green sky. Smart—and lucky, for Clyde Tombaugh, anyway; Clyde has big, big plans.

"Boy—your fork handle!" They're breaking for lunch, a threshing crew of eleven men, including the fourteen-year-old Clyde, and if you don't pack your pitchfork into the haystack handle-first, the grasshoppers always attack the wood. That gesture should have been second nature by now, so much of his life has been spent in working sixteen-hour days in fields like this, so much of him becoming a cog in the rhythms of Midwest farming. The family owned 250 acres, and he'd have been expected to know every stalk and husk of the season, in every row.

But occasionally he "got moony," as they called it. Or maybe "Marsy": even in Burdett, Kansas, out in the cow shit and clay, they know about the twentieth century; and lately, more and more, in his head the orange-reddish fields at sunset blur without resistance into the russet dunes of Mars.

He's born in 1906, the first of six children for Muron and Adella. The solar system has eight known planets. A thousand miles away from the world of wheat, at the Lowell Observatory, set like a gem in the highest of Arizona's peaks and pointed at its unobstructed skies, the famous Percival Lowell is one year into his patient and persistent search for "Planet X"—the ninth of the solar family that he's certain is in hiding out there.

Clyde is a good boy, industrious, polite, adept at smoothing the sometimes recalcitrant hitches in farm machinery. For threshers of wheat and huskers of corn and trudgers through mud in the wake of horse-drawn harvest wagons, the family is pretty much educated. (Jacob Tombaugh, Clyde's grandfather, was a schoolteacher who had completed college.) Clyde attends a two-room schoolhouse. He reads—he loves reading. At night, his body done stropping itself on the sharp edge of a day's hard work, he turns the pages of anything—anything that *has* pages—in the oleo-yellow light of his kerosene lamp. And his uncle Lee, on the farm only nine miles over . . . ? Lee has a three-inch-diameter nonachromatic reflector—a telescope! It's not unlike the primitive (but obviously effective) telescope Galileo had first used. 1918: Clyde peeks through it when he's twelve. And so his true life begins. The moon! He can see the moon! Its face is more ridged than his own fingerprints, more bumpy than his brother Roy's pimples. It looks as if he could grate cheese on that roughly textured surface! (If he trained this marvelous looking-tube on Annie Melcher's bedroom, *then* what mysteries would he—*no, don't think that!*)

By age sixteen his interest in the star-flecked sky is overwhelming. In order to observe, he needs to "dark-adapt"—to spend a prefatory hour adjusting his eyes in a darkened room. His brother Roy says, "He just sat there; he couldn't read anything, and we didn't have a radio or a phonograph." Biographer David H. Levy picks up the anecdote: "Clyde's mind was always so active that he had no trouble keeping it occupied during such a long wait. For instance, one day after farm work he calculated the number of cubic inches in Betelgeuse, the bright star on Orion's east flank: His solution was 1 duodecillion (39 zeros)." *In. His. Head.* (Another day, he calculated the number of kernels of wheat in a 10,000-bushel granary.) "Muron" (they're in bed whispering), "is that *our* boy, or did the fairies leave him?" "Don't worry none, Adella. I don't know *what* his future is, but he *has* one."

In the barn, when he's alone in the familiar darkness scented sweetly of sawdust and horse dung, Clyde can lean his groin against a rail and think of girls. They're so . . . you know, different! So enticingly different! He leans and he softly groans. They're so enticing . . . and they're about as distant from him as Neptune and Jupiter; farther maybe. Girls . . . and planets . . . Sometimes he dreams of Annie Melcher's stylish mother until her red, red lips are puckered into a circle that blends in his fancy into the high red circle-shape of Mars. So beautiful; so unexplored.

He reads, and excels. His schoolteachers favor him. David H. Levy assumes that Clyde knew Keats's exalting sonnet "On First Looking into Chapman's Homer," with its allusive burst of astronomical triumph. (In fact, the first chapter of Levy's biography of Tombaugh is titled "Looking into Chapman's Homer.")

> Much have I travell'd in the realms of gold
> > And many goodly states and kingdoms seen;
> > Round many western islands have I been
> Which bards in fealty to Apollo hold.
> Oft of one wide expanse had I been told
> > That deep-brow'd Homer rules as his demesne;
> > Yet did I never breathe its pure serene
> Till I heard Chapman speak out loud and bold:
> Then felt I like some watcher of the skies
> > When a new planet swims into his ken;
> Or like stout Cortez when with eagle eyes
> > He star'd at the Pacific—and all his men

Look'd at each other with a wild surmise—
Silent, upon a peak in Darien.

He's on fire with this. He reads, he joins some correspondence astronomy clubs (do girls belong?—maybe girls belong!), he sends for a copy of *Scientific American's Amateur Telescope Making*. Two dollars. "When a new planet swims into his ken." He looks up "ken." (He thinks of "ken" as a net, and planets as swimming puffer fish.) He saves up farm-chore money for the materials he learns he'll need. Uncle Lee can keep his trusty, rusty, creaky little ol' looker. Clyde's going to build his *own* telescope!

It's a wonderful age of how-to and know-how and autodidact twiddling. Darwin is in the air, electricity is in the wires, parts for a zillion amateur inventor projects are in the mail. Catalogs! Pen pals! Manuals!

Clyde sets up a grinding stand on a post dug into the ground just south of the house, and works on an eight-inch mirror—a "speculum"—that, because he lacks the professional skill to silver its surface, gets sent to the telescope firm of Napoleon Carreau in Wichita, Kansas. But, as Clyde says later, "Everything I did was wrong," and though Carreau is impressed by the young man's dedication, he has to report that the lens is pretty much a botch. What he needs, says Carreau, is an underground testing chamber, the kind the *real* backyard astronomers use. That part both stings and inspires: the *real* astronomers! What *is* he then, some cornpone kid just toying around at the grownfolks' table?

"Dad, we're doing so good, and we have so much *surplus* lately. Wouldn't a cellar be a help, for storage?"

"Well, sure it would be a help, Clyde. It would also be a goldang thing to dig. Now hand me that bag of nails there."

"Dad . . . And it would double as a tornado shelter. We *need* a tornado shelter. You said so yourself last year, when the hail-storm hit. You said . . ."

"I know what I said, boy. The question is, what are *you* say-ing? Under what you're saying, tell me the other thing you're saying."

After the 1926 harvest, Clyde begins the tough work, with his father's permission but by himself, on a cellar seven feet deep and twenty-four by eight. Some nights the wheelbarrow he muscled down and up and down the loading planks all day keeps making its wearying circuit in his sleeping brain until he wakes with a lingering image of loading and unloading heaps of dream dirt.

When the pit is finished, neighbors help pour twenty cubic pounds of concrete. Lordy! There's an arched roof, stairs, and windows. Even with the stacked-up dairy products and canned goods, it's a chapel for astronomy, it's a cool, calm, wingding wonder!

Up—the compulsion is up. And he's getting there, slowly, in hard-won stages. *Up.*

He just didn't know he'd have to shovel so damn far *down* to get there.

The second mirror, cellar-perfect, gets sent to Carreau for sil-vering in late spring of 1927. "A happy improvement by many degrees," he writes to Clyde, who accepts this sentence of praise as if a king of old had just knighted him. He views the impres-sive match-scratch of Comet Pons-Winnecke striking across the night sky. He begins a third telescope, grinding the Carbo-rundum with infinite patience, and then the polishing rouge; the mounting includes odd parts from his father's retired 1910 Buick and an out-of-luck cream separator.

Carreau sends a letter: in one year, he'll be needing an as-sistant, and if one Clyde Tombaugh would care to put his skills to work professionally . . . Well, *would* he! Would he ever! Meanwhile, by fall of 1928 he's making drawings of Mars, and then of Jupiter rotating on its axis. Are they good? Well, golly, *he* doesn't know, although he has his hopes, and late in December he mails his drawings to the astro-honchos at Lowell Observatory in Arizona, requesting suggestions for improvement. *Let* his brother Roy step out with that giggle-puss jiggle-tits Annie Melcher and come home caked in back-road dirt as if they'd rolled around out there like rutting hogs . . . okay, but Clyde is drunk on the wine of astronomy, Clyde is striding into the future wearing a sorcerer's star-burred cape, Clyde Tombaugh is opening up the sky like his personal cabinet of curios and arranging the planets like eight resplendent geodes on its shelves!

> *October 8, 1928*
> *Dear Mr. Tombaugh,*
>   *Dr. Lapland and I admired your drawings, particularly the Jupiter sample of July 7. Your letter arrives at an opportune time as we happen to have a position open at the moment for a man able to operate a new photographic telescope. . . . Would you be able to withstand long, cold nights in a mountaintop observatory? . . .*

At first the words are gibberish. Even the signature doesn't make sense, it's so plummeted into his afternoon from another cosmos altogether. *Yours, sincerely, V. M. Slipher, Director, Lowell Observatory.*

He slaps his hand on the envelope's postmark. Then he takes a deep breath and slowly, slowly spreads his fingers until the smeary telltale words are visible. *Flagstaff Arizona.* Really. Flagstaff Fucking Arizona. Oh Mr. Napoleon Carreau, I'm sorry. Oh corn and wheat and horse poop, good-bye.

And so on January 14, 1929—without even funds for a ticket

back home if his ninety-day trial period is a failure—Clyde Tombaugh boards the train for a twenty-eight-hour journey west.

He brings along plenty of reading: back issues of *Popular Science, Amateur Experimenter, Sky and 'Scope,* and a book of poems, although some of the latter he knows by heart and so he doesn't need them to read so much as keep nearby for a talisman.

Will he be true to his task, to his future? He looks out the window at night, and whispers.

Bright star, would I were stedfast as thou art—

3. JK

And he'd often lazily daydream back to those human planets pirouetting awkwardly over the schoolyard grass . . . *a solar system . . . a way of imagining form . . . (thus, understanding; thus, control) . . . upon the unthinkable Void.* In the wake of his mother's death (Keats was fourteen), in that inconsolable time, even the regularity of humdrum school routine seemed purposeful, a rescue. Biographer Denise Gigante: "Later in life, John would continue the habit of punctilious dressing in order to combat melancholy." As he put it, "Whenever I find myself growing vapourish I rouse myself, wash and put on a clean shirt, brush my hair and clothes, tie my shoe strings neatly and in fact adonize as [if] I were going out." Not eye-poppingly solar, perhaps, but . . . a system just the same.

"Ah you! My very own prince, to escort me and my newfound retinue to this beautiful view." The girl was flirting with him, Matthew Wynsome, medical student and self-styled rake, was pleased to see. Yes, flirting with him, as planned: it was the reason for delivering this gaggle of ten young chattering friends, with basketed wine and cold chicken, to an isolated overlook where the sea on its near end doilied itself at the foot of the cliff and, at its far end, dwindled indistinguishably into the sky.

"Indeed, milady, I endeavor to provide the view that the viewer herself deserves. Exalting induces exalting. And as for our fellow adventurers, let me introduce, with the pride of a royal chamberlain, Master Randolph, Mistress Millicent . . . ," and he casually named those sprawled nearby. His own companion's, he saw now, wasn't the only flirtation: overly courtly gestures from some of the men as they uncorked the wine, and overly coquettish side looks from the women.

"And who is he, with his back to us?"

"Sitting on the cliff edge there, milady? An introspecting

acquaintance of mine who, too, is from the great lists of the medical fraternity."

"But he has his back to us!"

"Well . . . yes. But he has his face set to the Infinite *[wink]*—eh, Johnny?"

In 1811, for a senior school prize, Keats was awarded a copy of John Bonnycastle's *Introduction to Astronomy in Letters to His Pupil,* an enormously popular book that was originally published in 1786 and stayed in print through 1822. Historian Richard Holmes says, "Bonnycastle's book was a thoroughly Romantic production, which included a good deal of 'illustrative' cosmological poetry from Milton, Dryden and Young." (Bonnycastle's publisher was also William Blake's and, later, Coleridge's and Wordsworth's.) "It also sported an engraved frontispiece by Henry Fuseli. This showed the goddess of astronomy, Urania, in a diaphanous observation-dress . . . instructing a youthful male pupil."

It's no surprise that Keats was enthralled by this book, and reread and reread it, and that the planetarium dome it made inside his schoolboy skull never dimmed. Its enthusiasms remained in there, all of the astral beacons and schoonering planetary globes that fill, or at least preside over, his writing. Bonnycastle gave Herschel's 1781 discovery of Uranus its own chapter, and we can see how Keats's memory of reading about that dramatic achievement surfaces five years later in his sonnet on "Chapman's Homer."

Nor, given his character, is it any surprise that the lesson the young Keats took from Herschel's discovery of Uranus wasn't that of laborious calculation, of painstaking and mechanical record keeping (although of course those were a large part of it), but that of the "Eureka!" moment: the revelatory light burst when a Seeker possessing determination and genius is crowned with success. Or, symbolically, the moment the goddess Urania exposes to him her most intimate of secrets.

In 1817 Keats and his brother Tom journeyed to Canterbury—Chaucer's city, with its castle grounds, imposing Gothic church, and old Roman garrison walls. Tom explored these. Keats was at work on *Endymion,* his first ambitious project, and had no time for mere sublunary interests, for mortals and their crumbling productions. In the poem he seeks happiness in a "higher hope . . . / of too wide, too rainbow-large a scope, / To fret at myriads of earthly wrecks." Gigante says, "Despite its magnificence, the ancient cathedral city and its great ruined castle captured his imagination less than the moon and the stars."

He was drawn to the sublime.

That is, he was drawn to explore the sensuality and what might be called the "empyrean" or the "cosmic," drawn to comprehend it in follicle, optic nerve, tongue root, and dendrite . . . that is, finally, he was drawn to attempt great poetry at what he believed to be its highest, most impassioned—and most demanding—level.

On December 28, 1817, Benjamin Haydon, painter of plush historical scenes, threw a festive dinner for the arts crowd in his north London studio. William Wordsworth was there, and Charles Lamb, and according to Haydon, "They abused me for putting [Isaac] Newton's head into my picture." (Newton was then known only to be the empirical, clinical man-of-scientific-calculation supreme; the mystical side of his character, which we know now, hadn't yet been uncovered.) Newton, the anti-artist, the exemplar of Reason over Imagination, and the champion of, as Richard Holmes says, "the destructive and reductive effects of the scientific outlook."

Lamb declared that Newton "believed nothing unless it was as clear as the three sides of a triangle." At which, an aspiring young poet named Keats chirped up to agree with Lamb that

Newton "had destroyed all the poetry of the rainbow." And then
the assemblage lifted their cups (far from the evening's first,
one supposes) and drank an ironic toast to "Newton's health,
and confusion to mathematics!" There was a rousing, resound-
ing cheer. It seemed to Keats as if the surrounding crowd in
Haydon's paintings—men in robes and armor from Christ's
Jerusalem, and the toga'd Romans from the days when the
pagan gods walked the Earth—joined in. There, in an oily-dark
corner . . . did one enthusiastic fellow lift his spear and shake it?
Did a priest-king wearing a shaggy pelt roar forth with the rest
of the revelers?

Heady stuff, this sublimity.

But it came with a price.

Sublimity requires hours-long lone looking off a cliff edge
into the transcendental murk on the horizon. It needs to drift
aloft. It can't be dully anchored by a chicken thigh provocatively
unwrapped from a basket and offered up by a woman with se-
ductive jabber in mind. If you're communing all night exclu-
sively with the Man in the Moon, you have no time for man.

Gigante reminds us of how "the 'voice mysterious' of the sea
calls out to him," how for Keats "the moon in her mythological
splendor peers out through a curtained sky"—surely a beckoning prospect—and yet how "elevated reverie, sustained thought
and intensity—combined with a constitutional inability to tol-
erate inauthenticity, either in oneself or in others—can make
for great poetry, but can also make the poet's path through life
more demanding."

Isolation is a two-edged state. The question behind Keats's
lifelong (and not consistently successful) balancing act, she says,
was "how to attain the sublime vision made possible through
solitude, and yet maintain the human connection necessary to
avoid that soul-killing vacuum, solipsism?"

There were nights, many nights, when the moon's full face

(or circumspect, wan part-face) didn't suffice, and Keats could look back even to the medical training he'd fled from once as a time when the human connection kept him tethered here, to the rest of us: A mother cuddling her new, ninth child, still with the blood petals dried to her inner thighs. A young man turned so that the wound in his rib cage looked to be the mouth the moaning issued from. A severed arm, a leg, still warm when Keats was asked to bear them out of the surgery room. The sweet stink of humanity was a cloud above the offal pail. It glued him to these other lives.

And if his embrace of sublimity sometimes made him question his life path, it made others question its place in his failing— and all too rapidly fatal—health. If you choose a goal that's all-consuming . . . by definition you get consumed. Keats didn't believe in this diagnosis himself (and he was correct in that), but felt obliged to send it along in a letter to his sister: "The Doctor assures me that there is nothing the matter with me except . . . the too great excitement of poetry."

There were aesthetic dangers as well.

He understood how, in his courtship of the sublime, a poem could waft away on Olympian clouds, or a gee-whiz pumped-up rush of adrenaline, and so be lost to the world of adult readers' adult concerns.

Part *one* of Wordsworth's definition of the creative act came readily to Keats, "the spontaneous overflow of emotion." Ecstasy welled up in his breast at the merest hint of a sunrise; brooding stalked him with the inescapability of his shadow. But the *second* part, "recollected in tranquility"—the search for a properly clarifying constraint—was the talent that needed growing into, and at first he often fumbled.

The major ingenue challenge he set himself in *Endymion* over-valued the constraint: he predetermined that this epic poem would be four thousand lines (a strangely numerical process for the sozzled young man who had boldly toasted "confusion to mathematics!"), and day by day, lodging by lodging (London, the Isle of Wight, Oxford, Canterbury, the "quaint coastal village" of Bo Peep, Paris, Hampstead, Burford Bridge . . .), he dragged the manuscript with him, ambitious and frustrated, needing to generate content enough to fill (and to be worthy of) the vasty expanse of that form.

He called the poem a "test, a trial of my Powers of Imagination and chiefly of my Invention . . . by which I must make 4000 Lines of one bare circumstance and fill them with Poetry." This sounds like strained production—manufactory, almost— and even though, as Mighall says, "there are moments of real beauty" (the sort of beauty implied in the poem's own opening lines: *A thing of beauty is a joy forever: / Its loveliness increases; it will never / Pass into nothingness*), still, "Keats has difficulty sustaining this over the course. . . . It fell short of his expectations and standards."

"Gelding," Keats said in a letter to his brother George, describing the process of his late revisions to the poem; no writer should have to speak so bitterly of his work. His final assessment (ironically, itself a tiny testament to Keats's knack for memorable language): "The foundations are too sandy."

And with that behind him, and greatness ahead, he entered the task of learning to govern the teeter-tottering back-and-forth of content and form. In a way, the story of his poetic success is the story of providing these two a viable mutual scale. With the completion of "The Eve of St. Agnes," says Mighall, "Keats manages a coherent synthesis of style and subject for the very first time. Intense sensualism and rich pictorialism . . . had been in abundance before, but their luxuriant excess, often for its own decorative sake, generally undermined argument or narrative. Here, finally, they are completely and successfully integral to his design." By the time of "the Great Odes . . . he found his voice and the perfect vessel for his mature artistry."

We can see him bent over the table, his head at rest on a manuscript page. It's night. The last gig of the street had sounded its weary clopping hours ago. The candle starts to stutter: it's as used-up now as this man. He looks so . . . *depleted*. And yet, if we could only stand behind him and read the lines he's just completed . . . *When old age shall this generation waste, / Thou shalt remain, in midst of other woe / Than ours, a friend to man, to whom thou say'st, / "Beauty is truth, truth beauty"—that is all / Ye know on earth, and all ye need to know* . . . we see it's more as if he's *decanted* the best of himself, into this.

"You're a good boy, John. No mother could ask for more. But you mustn't—" and then the phlegm-stuffed rattle-cough of a body becoming unjoined inside—"you mustn't attend me this faithfully. This journey I'm on will not be reversed by a forehead towel or a bowl of leeches." Still, she held out her hand and was grateful for his touch in return. He was fourteen. Does anything bring one closer to a mother than changing the pans; and lifting the spoons of broth; and reading to her as she's dying?

And that, she was. In March of 1810, at the age of thirty-five, the disease that already had taken her two younger brothers took Frances Jennings Keats.

But consumption (we would say tuberculosis) doesn't halt to revel in its victories. It keeps on. Opportunistic. Familial.

In December of 1818 Tom, the beloved younger brother, died just shy of his nineteenth birthday—again, after Keats's careful and affectionate attending to the seepages; and the coughs that rattle the bones like a butcher's cart; and the belly crawl of the spirit through ash and bloody spit-cloths and leech water. *Again*.

But twice isn't a form; twice is happenstance.

Infected mucus is highly contagious. On February 4, 1820, on "a [deceptively] mild day in a deep-frozen winter" (Mighall; Gigante says it was February 3), Keats spent the afternoon in London, without his bulky winter coat, and returned home to Hampstead riding on the outside seat of a coach, as he normally did for thrift's sake. Flushed and weak on arrival, he immediately went to bed. His friend Charles Armitage Brown heard the coughing.

"What is the matter, Keats?—you are fevered?"

"A little, yes, a little. Bring the candle now please, I want to look well at this blood. It is from my mouth." A single spot of it darkened the chilly white sheet.

This is what Brown's record says: "After regarding it steadfastly, he looked up in my face, with a calmness of countenance that I can never forget, and said, 'I know the colour of that blood;—it is arterial blood;—I cannot be deceived in that colour;—that drop of blood is my death-warrant;—I must die.'"

Three times is a form.

And as the bacillus thrived inside him, for the remaining twelve months of his weakening life, John Keats became the content of that form.

4. CT

Even in the zowier reaches of science fiction, the search for a planet is tedious.

Oh, if you want to stress the "fiction" part and downplay the "science," as many outer space wonder-romps do, it's possible to bypass the mind-numbing, painstaking labor. In another essay I've written about my lingering affection for the Doubles series of science fiction novels published continually by B-grade paperback publisher Ace from the 1950s into the '80s—those volumes in which two novels were bound together with one spine, topsy-turvy to each other (and so technically they had two front covers, and no backs). There were 221 Doubles sci-fi books in all (442 titles), and in most of them one can sense a spirit that thumbed its twenty-fifth-century nose at earthbound notions, lifted a gleeful middle finger to the breakable chains of gravity, and blasted gung-ho into a universe defined by adventureful gosh and devoid of numbers crunching.

James A. Corrick, in his overview study *Double Your Pleasure,* says, "The covers were often garish, the blurbs exaggerated, and the prose lurid." Once you've seen them lounging seductively on a drugstore spinner rack, there's no ignoring these books. That's what "lurid" means—it allures. Typical titles are *Sentinels from Space, The Universe Maker, Beyond Earth's Gates, The Stars Are Ours!, The Conquest of the Space Sea, The Forgotten Planet, Overlords from Space, The Space-Born, Space Station #1, Sargasso of Space, Empire of the Atom, The Cosmic Puppets, Voodoo Planet, Star Born, Planetary Agent X* . . . No day-at-the-office pencil tapping *here!*

But Isaac Asimov's science fiction ventures never depreciate the "science" half of the "science fiction" contract. In his novel *The Stars, Like Dust* (not published by Ace but Doubleday), Asimov's heroes are searching industriously for the "rebel world" they believe holds the key to overthrowing the tyranny of a galaxies-spanning "master race." But then he tells the reader, applying realistic brakes to his zoom-along warp-drive story,

> To those who have not actually been in space, the investigation of a stellar system and the search for habitable planets may seem rather exciting. . . . To the spaceman, it is the most boring of jobs. . . .
>
> Locating a star, which is a huge glowing mass of hydrogen fusing into helium, is almost too easy. It advertises itself. . . . But [and from this point on he may as well be writing about Clyde Tombaugh's task in Flagstaff] a planet, a relatively small mass of rock, shining only by reflected light, is another matter. One could pass through a stellar system a hundred thousand times at all sorts of odd angles without ever coming close enough to a planet to see it for what it is, barring the oddest of coincidences.
>
> Rather, one adopts a system.

There follow over two hundred words delineating this system, with no attempt to gild it with the fantastical. Then: "It is a very dull procedure indeed, and when it has been repeated three times for three different stars, each time with completely negative results, a certain depression of morale is bound to occur."

One understands why the Lowell Observatory panjandrums were pleased to hire a talented neophyte for this least compelling of observational projects. Founder Percival Lowell, millionaire and visionary, had died in 1916, leaving "Planet X" as yet undiscovered despite his enthusiasms and rigors. The quest continued, but sitting alone in the high cold dome, the whole night, every viable night, was a test of even a seasoned astronomer's dedication. And working the plates—"blinking" them, as the process was called—and comparing their complexities of star-dots (up to a *million* of them teeming on some of the individual goddam almost-alike exposure plates; and then the variables and asteroids!), image after image, pot of coffee after pot of coffee, patch of nebulosity after patch of nebulosity . . . eventually, one wore the look of a steer stunned by a two-by-four. But only give them a capable newbie, juiced up with a hard-on for the job, and willing to suffer the frosty air and the insufficient wages . . . Ah, here comes the train!

Then off to the observatory (Mars Hill, as they've named it), up a road so slick with the melting January snow that V. M. Slipher needs a second try before they reach the top. Hellos are tiny clouds of breath that visibly float in the chilly air. The first labor Clyde is assigned is furnace duty, tending to the split pine logs and each new night's 150 pounds of coal. Over two months of this sort of handymanning goes by; and then on April 6, 1926, once the observatory's new thirteen-incher lens is installed and a sample exposure is taken . . . Clyde Tombaugh officially tests the thumbscrews on each corner of the plates; and adjusts his eyepiece; and positions his feet; and smells the coffee, even as his nose hairs start to stiffen from the cold; and enters the boringest and fussiest-obsessive, pinhead-tabulating fool's job in the universe. But that's just it!—he's smack-dab *in* the void-and-fire glory ride of the universe, and he wouldn't trade this for anything.

Clyde Tombaugh's telescope is a battleship-worthy cylinder that declares its presence, its heavy bulky *hereness,* as soon as you see it. It's a reddish rust-orange (strangely, the color that conjures up not Pluto but Mars; and, not so strangely, a color that blinks between festive and—when linked in our minds to the unrelievable weight of its metal—industrial). In the photograph I'm looking at now it's pointed up at exactly that angle we laypeople always associate with sky exploration, with jaw-wagging, eye-goggling, dogged pursuit.

"Dogged"—if that even comes close. A time or two in that bubble above the rest of the world, Clyde's brushed by hypothermia. They'd provided him with a buffalo robe to wrap around his wiry string-bean body—the robe acquired from what old Arizona nook he never does learn—and he sits there feeling like some kind of half-beast priest-king shaman, arisen out of ancientdom to preside, here, now, on this unlikely throne. But that, and the hat with the earflaps, and the mummying sweaters, are still an insufficient fortifying. "Above the world," he hums to himself, "below freezing." The priest-king's mantra, in his battle against the basilisk cold.

And the rest of the world somewhere below his outlier perch continues its distant pursuits. There are nations relaxing, or festering, or making plans, between—although nobody sees it this way yet—two World Wars. There are eggs over easy being flipped at the Black Cat Café in downtown Flagstaff; some kissy-kiss or shoot-'em-up is playing at the Orpheum Theater. He has his suspicion that women of easy virtue (girls! somewhere on the planet are girls!) are sometimes smuggled into the other astronomers' quarters . . . or is that just a fevered imagining of his starstruck high-up hermitage? "Dogged"—yes. He's hounding the scent of something.

"Tombaugh's ten months of dedicated work would eventually yield 29,000 new galaxies, 3,196 asteroids, 1,800 variable stars, and 2 comets," Marcus Chown says in *Solar System*. I like that casual throwaway, "2 comets." Oh, right, two comets: *yawn*.

And one planet. Or what was then, in his lifetime, a planet, what was over seventy-five accepting years a planet, an icy grommet fastened to the firmament that I would have assumed was evermore a planet, as much a planet as Earth, as true as the seasons, as real as spring that faithfully returns every year with its

fruits and heifers and trilling streams when Persephone is con-
tractually released for those few months from the underground
halls of her husband—who happens to be, well, Pluto, a god,
an eternal.

And yet that planet I grew up with has been recently de-
moted. Knocked down to size. What reviewers did to Keats in
his knocked-down lifetime. Lord Byron famously said it was the
reviews that killed him. This may not give credit enough to tuberculosis, but we know what he means.

Still, Keats's poems survive. Not liking them is, as Joyce
Carol Oates once Twittered about *The Great Gatsby*, "Like spitting into the Grand Canyon. It will not be going away anytime
soon, but you will."

Certainly Keats doesn't go away from Clyde's star-sputtered
brain in his ten months of searching. If anything, they seem
to have occasional bursts of acquaintanceship, these oddball
two, seem to have anachronistic sightings of one another . . . as
if their eccentric orbits share a common nucleus, and time for
them isn't linear so much as sympathetic.

Why not? Keats had written his brother George in America
that, as Gigante summarizes it, "the present moment had no claim
on him. . . . When John and George opened their Shakespeare
at the same time, they might encounter each other." And Keats
wrote, "A Poet . . . has no Identity—he is continually in for—
and filling some other Body." Some nights, long nights, Clyde
feels filled for a moment. A line of Keats's comes out of the
great redundant sky, *O mortal pain! / O Darkness! Darkness!*, and
Clyde sees his shaggy-pelted self go floating across the ceiling
of that room in Rome as a body below, in hemorrhagic seizures,
thickly gasps its final moment.

And it's not as if Clyde hasn't turned his hand—at least when
he was a high school kid—to poetry. He can still (and on longer
nights, he does) recite "Our Team" from 1921. It begins

There's not a better team in the state!
We've beaten La Salle at any rate,
Pat slings his opponents around
Like a wind makes apples fall to the ground.

Then eight more lines for which, I think, it's best that only the stars are there to bear a silent witness.

5 · J^K

The recently widowed Mrs. Frances Brawne had rented one side of the house where Keats's friend Charles Dilke lived. With her: a fourteen-year-old son named Sam; a small girl, Margaret; and a daughter who had just turned eighteen, Fanny. Sometime in the late autumn of 1818 Keats and Fanny Brawne first met. They were just the right age, and about the same height.

Attraction thickened the air between them almost immediately, and they were together all of Christmas Day, whispering, sharing the coded stares that a simpatico couple develops over time. Fanny wrote it was "the happiest day I have ever spent."

Keats wrote, "Her nostrils are fine—though a little painful—her mouth is bad and good—her Profile is better than her full-face . . . —her feet tolerable . . . —monstrous in her behaviour flying out in all directions, calling people such names—that I was forced lately to make use of the term *Minx*."

Not exactly exemplary, ready-for-Hollywoodesque infatuation.

He'd written, "I hope I shall never marry . . . Though the most beautiful Creature were waiting for me at the end of a Journey or a Walk . . . my Solitude is sublime. . . . Nothing strikes me so forcibly with a sense of the ridiculous as love—A Man in love I do think cuts the sorriest figure in the world." He'd written, "When I am among Women I have evil thoughts, malice and spleen . . . I am in a hurry to be gone."

For what's become one of literary legendry's most cherished love stories . . . not exactly a promising start.

The challenge, as with his growing into his poetry, was one of structure. "Woman" was a form of the sublime for him, ideal in the way the shapes in Plato's Realm of Original Forms are ideal, supernal, and never disappointing: the Chair that's a pure idea of "chairness," the Bird that all birds on our mortal plane descended from and aspire to. (We're the defective counterparts of those perfect, immutable ur-selves.) For a form like that, the addition of content—dailiness in all of its squabble and Pap smear and stubble and drunken nuzzling and fraught misunderstandings—is only a violation. (One suspects this wariness came from a boyish fear, masquerading as a philosophy.) In an early poem, he writes,

> Shapes from the invisible world, unearthly singing
> From out the middle air, from flowery nests,
> And from the pillowy silkiness that rests
> Full in the speculation of the stars

—describing a level of Beauty so demanding, so constructed of Light itself, and of the Ineffable, that a woman might only exist there as a constellation, above a foot and its bunion, above a shrewish harangue with the costermonger. In a letter he says, "The mighty abstract idea I have of Beauty in all things stifles the more divided and minute domestic happiness."

And any coquette on a clifftop with a wink and a proffered chicken thigh? He imaged her as a way of trapping him into the domestic. To his publisher Keats once writes that "the love of a woman [is] treacle to the wings of independence." The more his heart was smitten (and yes, his heart *was* smitten), the more he argued *with* his heart. In his earliest surviving letter to Fanny (July 1, 1819) he tells her, "Ask yourself my love whether you are not very cruel to have so entrammelled me, so destroyed my freedom." From a later letter, this touching, revealing flash of self-awareness: "I am a Coward, I cannot bear the pain of being happy."

Pain was involved necessarily, and perhaps I wasn't fair when I attributed his obstinacy in the face of her charms to only "a boyish fear." Keats understood the financial precariousness of his bold leap from the medical profession to that of (always cap-P for him) Poet. He couldn't bear to provide her "Love in a hut, with water and a crust," and nothing more; she was stylish, she was deserving of fashion and comforts. Beyond that, of course, he intuited—below thought, in the folds of his lungs— that his future might be all too brief, a place "Where youth grows pale, and spectre-thin, and dies." If he was chary of anything deeper than casual dalliance, it was partly in the interest of saving Fanny from the dark world of insolvency—and the darker world of widow's wear.

And yet . . . And yet . . .

There they were. The sun through the fanlight, true to its point of entry, spread on the Turkish carpet in the shape of a peacock's opened tail. The house was quiet . . . except for Keats's heart, which sounded—surely anyone could hear it, even out in the street!—like cavalry.

He undid—she let him undo—a button. "This is how," he joked to himself in his head, "we derive the word 'button.' One, *but-one* only." His etymological jest was correct; she stopped him with a light touch, mixed of affection and rebuke. And it was this firmness in her, "a sudden bone in the butter" as he thought it, that created his growing respect for her; and then, out of the respect, a growing passion.

"I have been thinking, my Johnny . . ."

"Yes! And you *do* think, my love. I like that in you, ferociously. Brains and Brawne."

She arched a single eyebrow. "Oh, you are clever with language, sir! Have you thought of becoming a Poet?"

"What! A Poet? Not a Licentiate of the Society of Apothecaries? Not a Distinguished Member of the Royal College of Surgeons?" If he could have arched a responding eyebrow, he would have; but he lacked that power.

"Nor a tallow-chandler, or iron-monger, or cooper, or haberdasher, or uplands collier. Nor a King's Guard on a snow-white charger. No, I shall have you a Poet."

"And . . . ?"

"And you, my Johnny, will write your epics here by my side as fixed as a fork in a pothouse." (In those cheapest of taverns, the knives and forks were chained to the tables.)

"And . . . ?" Oh he was a duck in a pond of love, oh he was a smelt in a pan of the undying frying oils of love, oh he was dunked in love the way that the bathing machines at Margate dropped their holiday-makers *splash* into the sea.

"And, as I say, I was thinking . . ."—she let her eyes leave him, to circle the room—"I was thinking of how so impossibly large a fire as the Sun can be let through the fanlight there."

"And then?"

"It must be something in the way of how your Passions can be made to pass through a quatrain, my dear."

"That's so."

"Well then my love for you, although it's of immeasurable size, may also reveal itself . . ."

"Yes? Reveal itself?"

"Through only a single opened button, my love, which is for now sufficient."

Mighall claims that Keats's rapid turnabout in attitude occurred sometime in the autumn of 1818, not long after the finishing flourishes of his final Great Ode, "To Autumn," one of his last completed poems. The season, the poem says, "of maturing sun," the season to "fill all the fruit with ripeness to the core." These lines may have signaled a new corresponding maturity in himself.

In any case, says Mighall, "he visited Fanny on 10th October, and there immediately followed a string of ardent letters. . . . In the first he declared himself 'dazzled' by her, at 'her mercy,' and no longer resisting the tender yoke of love." Two days later the man who once wrote "I find that I cannot exist without poetry" writes Fanny that "My love has made me selfish. I cannot exist without you. . . . Love is my Religion—I could die for that—I could die for you. My Creed is love and you are its only tenet."

Perhaps a young woman inevitably is moved to return the loyalty of such a declaration. Perhaps she sensed ("I could die . . . I could die . . .") how little time remained for him—and something of a loving pity, or something in her in love with doom and drama, awoke. Perhaps she implicitly understood that in loving Keats now, earnestly, for this bespelled while, she did nothing to counter her chances for a more normal (and solvent) relationship in a future she had and he didn't. Perhaps he realized subconsciously that his major work was behind him now—the Nightingale, the Urn, and the rest—and his almost superhuman investment of passion was freed, to embody itself in earning her affections. Perhaps the priest-king flashed through his mind's back door, the shaman in the animal robe, and for just that single wingbeat of time he heard as if ancestral wisdom, "The one right kiss done right outweighs a scuttle-full of stars."

So many perhaps. Or it could be so simple as He + She = Wow, the ages-old formula that's passed down in the genes.

What we do know is that, as Mighall puts it, "the couple made their emotional commitment in a secret engagement." Gigante calls it "a private understanding."

And as the dying waxed inside him, his loving waxed apace. As the time moved on, their insouciant cooey banter was like the sparkling designs that skaters slice into ice above unacknowledged depths beneath.

In February, following the hemorrhage that Keats termed his "death-warrant," Charles Brown offered to the poet his front parlor, where Keats then spent the rest of that winter under a blanket before the fire. Brown chose, Gigante says, to be "fierce in enforcing the doctor's orders [for strict calm]. . . . Fanny Brawne had to make do with seeing her lover through his window." When

Brown left on errands she would sneak inside and sit by Keats, doing her needlework.

And when later, in June of 1820, he was found vomiting blood, and his good friend Leigh Hunt took him in ("heaving in pain, and horrible convuls'd") for around-the-clock nursing, "he slept much of the day," Gigante says, and "when not asleep, he would stare in the direction of Hampstead, thinking of Fanny."

The Leigh Hunt household, overrun by a brawling brood of children and rowdy literary lounge-abouts, proved impractical for an invalid's needs. Seven weeks from his arrival there, Frances Brawne took him in and "defied societal convention to let her daughter nurse John." The broth. The cool cloth to the forehead. The soiled underlinen. And over it all, the continuing blithe avowals of lovers' commitments. "In pity give me all," he'd written to her in a poem; "Withhold no atom's atom or I die."

But not the gift of every atom in Fanny Brawne's body could halt that march. His friend John Reynolds reported, "He is advised—nay ordered—to go to Italy." As if the atoms of the Mediterranean light could do what Fanny couldn't. Keats knew that his upcoming death was a fact, and yet—for everybody's sake—he needed to live by the fiction. Not long after, on September 13, 1820, the brig *Maria Crowther* was voyaging John Keats, heartbroken, Italy-ward.

Gigante: "During their final days together, Fanny had made every effort to pretend that the couple would be seeing each other again in the spring. . . . She clipped a lock of her hair for him as a keepsake, and she lined his traveling cap with silk."

"And Johnny . . ." Nobody else was around. She slipped something into his chill hand. Then she bent to kiss his brow. "I will be waiting for you when you come home, love."

In his palm were five torn-off buttons.

*

Later that day, an errand boy approached Wentworth Place. He recalled,

> I could n't resist going around to the kitchen door to
> ask after Mr. Keats, for I had n't seen him for a long
> time tramping around. It was September, and the back
> door was half open, and just inside Miss Brawne herself
> talking to one of the maids. I stammered out my words
> not feeling sure of my welcome, some way. Her answer
> was curt enough, but I have always fancied she'd been
> crying.

In private. In private only. Her content was nakedly grievous; but decorum dictated her form.

6. CT

Wilson Tucker's *To the Tombaugh Station* originally appeared in the July 1960 issue of the *Magazine of Fantasy and Science Fiction* (classified as "a short novel" on the cover and "a long novelette" on the contents page—an exquisite parsing of size). The plot revolves around Kathy Bristol, a spaceways bounty hunter in 2009, so far from 1960 into the future that, of course, a trip to Pluto is easily doable.

I would have been twelve when that issue appeared on the stands, and "Tombaugh" would have been only a strange name. Now I know enough to see the small honorific involved in Tucker's naming one of Pluto's plateaus (and therefore the astronomical observatory station on it) after the planet's discoverer. In fact, Tucker envisions the Tombaugh Station as clearly in the spirit (and the physical conditions) of Clyde Tombaugh's own night-by-night experience: it's an isolated pod of a place, set in a landscape of bone-white escarpments and fatal cold, its telescopic capability ever alert to the universe beyond. (Is it coincidence that Isaac Asimov's science column on page 65 of this same issue is called "Beyond Pluto"? He starts, "A couple of days ago [as I write] a Soviet astronomer announced the discovery of a tenth planet, one beyond Pluto." A mistake; but even so, it's in the spirit of Tombaugh's impulse.)

Not long after this original appearance, *To the Tombaugh Station* appeared as number D-479 in the Ace Doubles series, with a striking Valigursky cover of bubble-helmeted spacemen afloat against the ebony endlessness, and backed (or fronted, depending) by Poul Anderson's kitschier-covered *Earthman, Go Home!* In kind and in chunkette length, *To the Tombaugh Station* was a natural for Ace to reprint. I note, though, that originally its opening was matter-of-fact: "Kathy Bristol entered her supervisor's office by the side door." Its redone Doubles version starts: "She was a huntress . . . in a statuesque body."

Ah, Ace, Ace, Ace . . . what *would* my adolescence have been without you?

I've been thinking of a new Ace Double. One side is a life of Keats (it's the shorter of the two sides). On the cover a young man, wide-eyed, almost deliriously enthused with life, is walking under a deeply indigo sky that's ablaze with a nervous system of stars: "He dared to voyage to the sublime!" The other side is a life of Clyde Tombaugh. On the cover a young man, wide-eyed, almost deliriously enthused with life, is—well, we'll add a 1920s thresher in the background to distinguish this from the other, with moonlight glimmering off its levers and blades. "They said he couldn't, but he reached the solar system's edge!" On both of the covers the sky is a thing of overcompelling mystery in a way that implies our life here on Earth is, as well.

They're two different stories. And yet, placed thus, they share a spine.

And so I can't refuse the thought of that frequently relied-upon sci-fi trope, the wormhole. How many novels and movies and comic books and video games by now have used the dubious but popular idea of this tunnel through the fabric of space: your rocket cruiser enters it at one end and, in a blink of the spacetime continuum, you exit at the other end a gazillion light-years distant. It allows the creation of stellar-expansion empires, and of import-export systems as vast as a galaxy, and of cops-and-robbers played along the dangerous alleys of nebular drift. And information—from one world to another, almost as speedy as thought!

So now I'm placing an actual *bookshelf* wormhole into my two-title book. With paper now half a century old, that's not un-likely. Keats and Clyde—a corridor of narrative trade between the two. Keats and Pluto, Clyde and Fanny, corn husks, lung blood, night sky like a blessing and an imprecation settling into the single era and onto the single continent where we all live, at our most rhapsodic . . .

For better or worse, I've always been susceptible to what sci-fi novelist John C. Wright suggests in his novel *Orphans of Chaos:* "The argument was incomprehensible, and that made it easier to believe."

I've always felt the truth of these enchanted lines in a poem of Gregory Orr's:

> Sometimes, entering
> The house of a poem,
> You're greeted
> By your other self—
>
> That person you
> Could have become
> Had things gone
> Differently.

June 7, 2013 / 2:20 p.m.

The 1800 block of Palisade Street in Wichita, Kansas, is given over to lower-income single-family houses—although who knows what inventive versions of "family" really live in them? Most have a slightly frowzy, but not unappealing, aspect.

Some, like the red-faced fat kid valiantly straining for some success at a chin-up bar, are obviously holding on to a sense of respectability and are trying to lift themselves higher than that: a second job, an English-as-a-Second-Language night course, a Bible study group.

Others, it's not unreasonable to guess, are holding on to a basement meth lab. One or two of the teenage girls know how to squeeze twenties from the wallets of lower-end horny businessmen.

In early June, the trees are greenly lush enough to bump

boughs with the corresponding trees on the other side of the street; they form a spotty, rustling, block-long canopy that sieves the light, which lands with an attractive dappling effect.

I park in front of 1836. It's small, and one of the frowzier, a bunker-like construction sided cheaply with thin aluminum slats. A faded-yellow child's plastic chair sits on the concrete-slab-of-a-front-stoop, and beside it is an overturned plastic bucket, enervated-blue. An empty minivan waits on its minimal concrete apron.

I'm making notes—these notes that you're reading. Suddenly the front door thutters open and a girl, about five or six, skips out, with the bounce of her frizzy ponytail exaggerating her energy. I've been up since eight, and her eyes are the alivest things I've seen all day, quick and huge with an innocent curiosity. Her skin is that butternut-cocoa color America is tending toward as formerly inviolate races and nationalities mix in sexual tra-la-la. One day her ass may be cooling in a jail cell, on a drugs charge. Then again, one day she may be in the Oval Office, determining national policy.

An option that no sane person could have imagined for her in 1926.

In that year, optometrist and telescope maker Napoleon Carreau was living at, and conducting his business at, this address. And that was the year an eager farm boy from Burdett, Kansas, sent his carefully ground and polished eight-inch speculum to Carreau, to have it professionally silvered.

Whatever house Carreau lived in, it wasn't this cheaply thrown-together 1960s aluminum block. I have no idea how many structures have stood on this lot since 1926, as we have no idea what would have become of Clyde Tombaugh had he accepted a life of employment here . . . but one suspects his name would just be yesterday's flown-away thistledown; gone with the wind; writ in water.

This girl from 1836 is staring at me in my Nissan with a problematic combo of focused interest, open willingness to converse, suspicion, and territoriality. I don't know her real future any more than I can posit Tombaugh's alternate-reality 1826 Palisades future; but I can feel the uncontrollable wild exuberant girlish oomph in her—her content—and I hope the form it finds one day is as functional for her as the sky that finally shaped his crazy wheat field dreaming was, for him.

And Clyde's "real future"? It will be an exemplary thing. He'll meet Patsy. They'll be married for sixty-two affectionate years. The children. The satisfying career as a teacher. The grandchildren. Fund-raising. Autographs. The honorary coaching of varsity football at New Mexico State. At age eighty-two he'll still be on the lecture circuit; at Stellafane Observatory, three thousand knowing astronomy buffs will deliver a standing ovation before he orates a single word. When he slumps over dead in his wheelchair on a Friday morning in 1997, and the announcement is issued, dozens of editorial cartoonists walk around all day with an image in their heads of a full-faced Pluto shedding a tear.

But nobody knows this in 1930. There's no telescope for future time. Clyde knows that the day is cold and cloudy: February on Mars Hill. At the Orpheum Theater, Gary Cooper's seminal western *The Virginian* is playing. Clyde's eyeballs feel as tight as a military bedsheet, and gritted—nothing new about that. He aligns the blink comparator plates from a few days earlier, January 23 and January 20. And checks. *Don't get TOO woowoo excited, farm boy.* And double-checks. And triple-checks. And then he walks down the corridor past the secretary's room, to the large main office, and knocks, and enters, and utters some of twentieth-century science's most amazing words: "Dr. Slipher, I found your Planet X."

He says that aloud; in his head it's all *woowoo*.

And then? A bout of caution. As Clyde says, "Everybody was excited as the dickens!" but nobody wants to rush. It isn't until mid-March that the International Astronomical Union's Central Bureau in Copenhagen distributes the imprimatured news to the world that it spins about in a system of planets newly numbered at nine.

And the flashing of the cameras, and the amazing rivers of (pink *and* gold!) champagne, and the thousands of letters suggesting a name for the system's newcomer. Headlines, busybody gawkers, generals, mayors, pundits, comedians, gushing women (girls!), and enough hands to shake in a day to last a Kansas kid a lifetime.

There's a particularly important press convening at the telescope itself, and the observatory staff is there with its range of emotions from stuffy pride to Clyde's astonished shyness. One reporter—and a brassy, beautiful woman she is, too—asks him, with a discomforting unblinking look, how it happened, how it felt, what it was like "to father a planet."

"Well, ma'am, it just swam," Clyde tells her with a secret smile, "into my ken."

7. AG

Bronze and springily flexible and eleven inches long (and looking something like an engine's dipstick, with a charming insect-body handle and a horizontal splash guard), the elegant subject captured in this photograph is improbably but actually the proboscis of an insect . . . the sphinx moth from Madagascar.

Its wings are a velvety mottle of fawns and cocoa-browns and bumblebee-like gold-and-black-brown nap. And even in Madagascar, where it *isn't* "exotic," it's still considered exotic. With a proboscis extended three times the length of its thorax, it certainly earns the aura of mystery that its name implies, the name that European entomologists gave it upon discovering it fluttering through the sunlight of the mothways with the utter unfathomability of a sphinx.

Darwin had predicted its existence decades earlier, while studying an example of a Madagascar orchid from a botanical collection right in England.

Spectral, spindly, and a richly waxy white, the flower offers up to the world an outsized eleven-inch nectar receptacle. *Something* had evolved in Madagascar to effectively harvest that nectar, yes? To hover with pinpoint grace above it, to make an aerial obeisance, a thrust, to effortlessly perform what Keats was longing to perform as he sat on a dockside staring into the clammying scumble of the bay's incessant clouds, wherein a loose mélange of Fanny Brawne and poetry, and poetry and Fanny Brawne, enacted the wedding of content sliding perfectly into form until it *became* the form—and the wedding of form, opening, and accepting, and closing holistically over the content.

How they dance around each other, these two! Bumping, parting, looking moodily anywhere *but*, then approaching again, daring a tango step or two, then dancing cheek to cheek, then parting again . . .

It wasn't uncommon for the seventeenth-century nouveau riche in England to invent long-standing pedigrees, sometimes to the point of exhuming an actual ancestor's bones—a fishmonger's, say—and reburying them below a marble bust in a more prestigious churchyard. / *form with bogus content*

The annual Cheese Rolling competition in Gloucester has been held since 1850, but in 2010 the traditional eight-pound wheel of Gloucester cheese was replaced by a plastic one. / *seemingly stable form, but altered content*

On April 4, 2013, a pair of bloody eyeballs packed in ice was found in a box set on the lid of a trash bin across from the pumps of a Kansas City, Missouri, gas station: pigs' eyes, it was determined, but no other information was ever found out. / *mystery content, separated from its original form*

The current human genome contains a small amount of Neanderthal code, on average about 2.5 percent. / *form with generally unacknowledged content*

Father Gabriel Amorth, head of the International Association of Exorcists, claims to have carried out 50,000 exorcisms, sending 160,000 demons out of human bodies and back to Hell. / *form with metaphysical content*

After routine prostate surgery in 2009 in a German hospital, Dirk Schroeder's X-ray revealed sixteen pieces of medical equipment left inside him, "including a needle, a six-inch roll of bandage, a compress, several swabs and a fragment of surgical mask." / *form filled by accidental content*

A group of miners shot dead when they attacked police at the Lonmin platinum mine in Marikana, South Africa, had used a potion made from the tongue and chin of a murdered security guard to render them bulletproof. / *content that fails to sustain the form*

Foster E. L. Beal, in the employ of the U.S. Bureau of Biological Survey early in the 1900s, spent much of his twenty-five years there slicing open the stomachs of 37,825 birds ("with particular attention to the woodpecker branch"), examining the food in their guts to determine which birds were "good" and which were "bad" for the nation's agriculture. / *obsessive hunt through form for its contents*

Data from the IceCube neutrino telescope shows that two neutrinos under study "each had energies of about 1 petraelectronvolt." / *impossible-to-imagine form with impossible-to-imagine content*

And so goes the dance, and so goes the dance.

And Keats and Clyde? With no overt attachment, I've attached them here. I've needed them, two characters in search of a common essay. That's the form, and I've asked them to step inside it, from out of their independent lives and from under their independent heavens: I've reminded them that Pluto was discovered in the Gemini constellation (the Twins); and I've read to them about how photons of light can be made "entangled" and act as one although separated by hundreds of miles; I've asked them to try to be a working binary system for this little while, to take a ticket and enter the tango line and see what happens.

8. JK

> The calmest thoughts come round us; as of leaves
>> Budding—fruit ripening in stillness—Autumn suns
> Smiling at eve upon the quiet sheaves—
> Sweet Sappho's cheek—a smiling infant's breath—
>> The gradual sand that through an hour-glass runs—
> A woodland rivulet—a Poet's death.

Three years ago he had written this, three years before the night that first dark ominous spot of lung blood appeared on his sheet. In a sense, what he had to do now was complete the shape he'd worked at constructing all of his life, filling it in.

They were standing on deck, leaning against the rail. Heading out to sea on a clement day, with the sky and the water vying for the prize of most lucent blue. Masted sails scattered along the horizon, like laundry hung from an invisible line.

"A long way, John. I feel as if we may as well be voyaging to Timbuctoo."

"Ah, Severn . . . ! I'm afraid I am voyaging much, much farther than that."

Joseph Severn accompanied him. Severn was a budding artist (he'd won some medals already) and later admitted that, at first, his easy willingness to serve as the traveling companion of his old school friend John Keats was motivated at least in part by hopes for his own career—Rome *was*, after all, the acknowledged artistic capital of the world. But over the months of Keats's wasting there, Severn met the deeper occasion with a consistent, unflagging empathy that Mighall calls "as gratifying in its untiring selflessness as the details of what this entailed are harrowing."

Just the crossing was a harrow blade or two.

For six weeks, Keats and Severn shared their cabin space with the captain and two difficult female passengers: a fussy martinet named Mrs. Pidgeon; and Miss Cotterell, a frail adolescent who was also in an advanced stage of consumption, and who, when not in a faint, would argue with Keats over whose condition appeared to be least or most dire. The ship was often becalmed ("a Flat day," Severn called these). At other times the water ran rough enough to rise like cliffs, and they would skidder down these as their gorge flew up in counterpoint; one morning as a cabin boy attempted to hold the breakfast table steady, a ham shot into Severn's lap. The bunks were frequently drenched, the chairs and trunks sent clattering around the overpopulated crypt-of-a-cabin like peas in a jester's rattle. Miss Cotterell needed the cabin window open, for air; Keats needed it closed against the chill. Twice, they were halted by other ships for questioning: once a quadruple-decker Portuguese man-of-war, and once a British warship. Miss Cotterell desired diverting merriment; Keats desired philosophical silence. And when they entered the Bay of Naples the ship was put into ten days of quarantine. The projected four-week crossing had lasted two months, some of it punctuated by Keats's vomiting blood. "I wish for death every day and night to deliver me from these pains, and then I wish [this] away, for death would destroy even those pains which are better than nothing. . . . The thought of leaving Miss Brawne is beyond every thing horrible." One morning Severn stood at the rail admiring the wake of the ship, silver in the sapphire water, following them—as if to taunt Keats—like a bridal dress's train.

Nor did arrival in Italy ease their distresses.

Today of course the rooms at 26 Piazza di Spagna above the Spanish Steps are a shrine to the poet who died there thinking his life was a waste and his poetry a failure and his reputation "writ in water"; thousands make their pilgrimage there each year. The tour buses come and go. But at the time, that stony building was simply the place where the dying—a painfully messy dying—continued, agonizing day by day. Keats's second-floor bedroom window gave onto a view of the Fontana della Barcaccia, the "sinking boat." That language would not have been lost on him. His attempt to study Italian by reading Vittorio Alfieri's tragedy *Filippo* came to a sudden end at the lines "Miserable me! No comfort remains to me / But crying, and that is a crime." The book was too much a mirror, and he tossed it across the room. And Fanny's final letters remained unread. Even the sight of her handwriting on the envelopes was a torture. "Oh, God! God! God! Every thing I have in my trunks that reminds me of her goes through me like a spear."

There were occasional lighter glimmers. Severn, with an optimism their future didn't warrant, set up his easel in the alcove off Keats's bedroom. Keats encouraged him to paint, and to venture out on his own: museums, cathedrals, street circuses, ladies fair! In their earliest days in Rome they even attempted some festivity as a duo—and why not? The mild clime was going to work its panacea magic on Keats's system! The grounds of the great Monte Pincio park were a beautiful medley of greenery where, as Keats's physician put it by way of recommendation for healthful strolling, "all of the beauty and fashion of Rome [come] to parade, either in their equipages or on foot, and discuss the gossip and tittle-tattle of the town." There was the Basilica of Saint Peter, "where a hundred lights were kept burning around the tomb of the saint." One day they went to the Borghese Palace, and there, with the special permission of the Princess Pauline Borghese (Napoleon Bonaparte's youngest sister), viewed the statue for which she had posed nude from the waist up, lounging seductively on a one-armed settee.

At a lighter cough, Severn would even joke. "Keats, don't be catching a cold, sir!" To which Keats would reply, more grimly and yet with levity still, "Severn, you may as well tell a man to not take a gulp of water as he walks the streets of Atlantis."

And all the while, although invisibly, death rotted away his inner foundations. Death's inducement: *I can end this endless terror.* Death went at him as at a suckbone, gnawing him, working its tongue in, teasing out the juices.

Eventually Keats couldn't accompany Severn out of his invalid's cell, and eventually Severn's sympathies wouldn't allow him to strike out solo. "Poor Keats . . . opens his eyes [from sleep] in great horror and doubt—but when they fall upon me—they close gently and open and close until he falls into another sleep—The very thought keeps me by him until he dies." Was it a thousand years ago that Severn had won the Royal Academy's gold medal for a painting called *The Cave of Despair?* He lived in it now.

"Keats?" he'd ask, solicitously.

"Severn . . ." It burbled out, toward the end, as if from a tar pit.

Toward the end, Keats wrote to Charles Brown, "There is one thought enough to kill me—I have been well, healthy, alert, &c, walking with her—and now . . . I am leading a posthumous existence."

On the tenth of December, Keats vomited a pint of blood, dark and syrupy. He was, wrote Severn, "more prepared for his death than I was." For two more months the hemorrhagings, those way stations of dying, became a fact of life.

On the night of February 21, Severn heard strenuous gurgling issue from Keats's throat. The poet asked him if he had ever seen anyone die. No, he replied. "Well then I pity you poor Severn—what trouble and danger you have gotten into for me—now you must be firm for it will not last long—I shall soon be laid in the quiet grave."

"But," Gigante says, "when the sun came shining through the window the next morning, and he was still alive to see it, John dissolved in tears."

And at 11:00 p.m. on February 23, he died in Severn's arms.

His body was wrapped in a winding sheet. His unopened letters from Fanny Brawne—as if some sonnet was tidily brought to closure in its final line—were placed above his heart.

At the end, are we vouchsafed a vision of our entire life brought up to that moment, a clear shape? Oh, we know what was *in* us: the hurly-burly pourings of thought and emotion we broadcast hither and yon, the cinctures of abstemiousness and the huge voluptuary excesses, the dreams that succeeded as well as the nose-dive dreams in hundreds of fragments, the whoop-ass, the bubble of quietude, *all* of the human bouillabaisse, olla podrida, and haggis that we call a life . . . but do we see the final *shape* all this will have made? As the poet Stephen Dunn asks, "Who were you, and who was I? / Such questions seemed like a lifelong job."

In an essay on Las Vegas brothels, Ginger Strand considers that city's well-remunerated sex professionals who flicker from being Ellen or Wanda or Margaret to being Allure and Honey Dew and Mistress Stern and then back. "Jocelynne" drives ten hours to the Bunny Ranch for her high-dollar gigs: "I need that ten hours to go from being soccer mom to being Jocelynn." Strand says, "Academic sociologists Barbara G. Brents, Crystal A. Jackson, and Kathryn Hausbeck . . . point out that the global economy's shift to selling experiences, things like themed travel, preprogrammed adventure, or fantasy [think of role-playing games and their wizard/sorceress avatars], has played into . . . [how] we have grown comfortable seeing ourselves as multiple. We're one person at work, another on Facebook, another in bed with a lover. In fact, there may not even be a 'real' self at the center, just endless new versions."

We're serial us. And surely this chimes chummily with a post-Newtonian quantum-mechanical cosmos where a subatomic particle seems to heckle our comprehension, zinging in and out of "impossibly" differing simultaneous states of subexistence;

where we're mainly a field of energy always redoing itself in emptiness.

Keats knew what's still today our common understanding of how this works on the cellular level: "I dare say you have altered," one letter says. "Every man does—our bodies every seven years are completely fresh-materiald."

He made it to three and a half of those sequential selves. Did he sense, in that near-to-final moment as Severn helped turn him to the sun, his priest-king guardian spirit appear from some future world, from some sky-scanning aerie, with a summary of those twenty-five years and their promiseful accomplishments?

Perhaps. And when he closed his eyes, was it then, along with his eyelids, that the lid of his life clicked shut, like a jar, like an ancient Egyptian canopic jar with the holdings of the mortal body inside it, in its darkness? Perhaps. As always: so many perhapses.

And perhapses aren't answers. Nor are these kinds of questions answerable.

But the light was a fact, and it bathed his face. The light was an incontrovertible fact, and it's been here, either obviously or covertly, in all eight sections of this essay. It bathed his face and perhaps . . . perhaps . . . he could feel it as we know it to be, the all-irradiant vehicle of delivery *and* the substance being delivered . . . in one. The perfect marriage: photon and ray, purely bodiless energy even as it carries the whole of our solid, embodied world. They bathed his face, this form and this content, married in the physics and the poetry, in the flesh and the spirit, they bathed his face like a consecration, in sickness and health, for richer or poorer, married until the eventual death of the solar system do them part.

The End of Space

The sky-car sailed quietly through the night of old Tschai,
over landscape ghostly in the light of the blue moon.
Reith felt like a man drifting through a strange dream.
He mused over the events of his life—his childhood, his
years of training missions among the stars and finally
his assignment to the *Explorator IV*.

// JACK VANCE, from *Tschai, Planet of Adventure*

1.

When the sky cracks open—the night sky, shattered to jagged
pieces by lightning—you can see, or at least you *think* you see, the
nanosecond glimmer of another world. A shiver passes through
the house's joists. And when the storm clears, and the clouds get
swept away like dust balls . . . there it is, that panoply of shimmer-
ing beacons set against the indigo deep. It's magical. Even here,
in the city, where every neon bar sign is a photon-rich competi-
tor, and accumulation of city light is an assault . . . even here, in
Wichita, Kansas, even now, in 2012, the sky reminds us that the
ancient-most mysteries still have the power to shirr the blood.

This means we can *almost* imagine what celestial terror and grandeur meant in the lives of our cave-dwelling ancestors. What a sudden bolt of lightning meant before the *idea* of "lightning." How that vast inhuman gorgeousness must have absorbed their limited gaze—their pupils like two drops lost in an ocean.

This was so early, they might have still thought that in a day or two you could walk there. Later on, its physical separateness would have been clearer; and then begins the dream, or the protodream, millennia before Da Vinci's contrivances, of visiting there, as the birds do.

Fly to me, fly to me.
Be more. Fly to me.

Up—the compulsion is up. The ancient priest-kings on their ziggurat tops, as close as they could lift themselves to the astral-studded bodies of their gods. The sky charts of pharaonic Egypt. Chichen Itza. In 600 BC Nebuchadnezzar builds his palatial tower "mountain high, of bitumen and baked bricks." If the myths of Greece conduct us deep and in—I'm thinking the Minotaur, the beast-man in his (presciently Freudian) labyrinth-subconscious— they will also lead us up and out: is any story more enthralling than that of Bellerophon coasting the sky on Pegasus? A horse—on wings! A horse as celestially, loop-de-loopily graceful as an eagle riding its currents! And Daedalus rises, just as kinds of wings more spiritual than his wax ones will, in the later stories, lift God's Son (and, later still, the Mother) up to Heaven. George Herbert makes the literal flying behind the Ascension explicit in his "Easter Wings," a poem in the shape of two wings, with its skylarks, and its image of "imping" taken from the vocabulary of falconry.

The yarmulke of the Jews serves as a constant tactile reminder that God is above. Above; but in contact—silken contact—with our heads. Above; but teasingly close. Unknowable; but attainable. A small cloth dome, like a planetarium dome, for every one of His Chosen People.

Be more. Fly to me.

But built into even the earliest stories is skepticism and, often, disaster. *Dis-aster:* "against the stars." Nebuchadnezzar's Tower of Babel is blasted to biblical smithereens. Daedalus's son falls into the sea. For all of his airborne glory, he's finally no more than a clawful of tripe let go of by some passing gull.

2.

And we sent John Glenn into orbit . . . why? We muscled up our techno-savvy and sent Buzz Aldrin and Neil Armstrong rocketing to the lunar surface ("Very very fine grained . . . almost like powdered charcoal") . . . why, exactly?

Well, for the pure eye-popping wonder, of course. For the magic. Ray Bradbury puts it neatly, remembering the thrill of being nine and coming upon—in 1929—the first Buck Rogers comic strip. "The enemy of every boy is gravity, and here in the first few days of Buck Rogers that incredible stuff 'inertron' plucks us off our feet and hurls us through the sky, free at last. And free not only to jump over dogs, rivers and skyscrapers, but to challenge the stars."

The electro-minaret palaces of the Emperor of Mars! The pleasure cars that ride the hundred-mile-drop "gas waterfalls" of Jupiter! The singing crystalline spheres that wake the deserts at dawn on Mercury! . . . The jaw-dropping polychromatic images brought back by the Hubble Telescope seem an adult, "real-world" validation of these youthful fictional marvels.

And so, yes . . . wonder. We did it for wonder. And for science. We believe in knowledge: what could be more beautiful than *that?* But surely, following *Sputnik,* politics and jingoism and ego and competition and territoriality—sum these up as fear—count too, as motivating forces. Serious Western strategists in the Cold War "space race" climate believed the rumor that Russian rockets were being prepared to reach the moon and spray it completely Communist-red as a nightly sign of domination.

They were going to *paint the moon*??? And we *believed it*??? Maybe a "sapiens" species like ours is innately doomed to have its most aerial aspirations forever flawed, forever limited—or quarantined?—to the planet on which we blunder about, cursing and conniving and picking our lips and tripping shlemiel-like over our laces.

3.

Her history training was thin; it was a lining that sometimes showed through a rent in the thicker outer layer of math and science. But she knew enough to realize that, having been born near Plymouth, Massachusetts—in that house like a great white wedding cake, tiered and swagged, on the top of the hill—her stroll right now along the California coast sands had her completing a journey that retraced what could be called America's journey, ever westward, until it gave out at the edge.

"It's time to go to sleep, Stella," her mother would say, and tuck her in, and sing her favorite song. That was thirty-five years ago. The divorce and the hysterectomy ago. And she'd look out the window—fighting sleep—at the spangled sky that, in her hilltop's smokeless air, was alive with a beautiful scintillant writhing. *One day I'll travel there,* she told herself.

But then, she thought she'd have children of her own too. That was before the hysterectomy. *Another space closed off to me.*

It glittered and pulsed and went on forever, ice-points and hellfire concretizing the otherwise empty black of utter endlessness, and it called her name, and it waited for her, and it lulled her into good-girl sleep.

Twinkle, twinkle, little star.

4.

In eighteenth- and nineteenth-century American paintings of the westward expansion, the travel is almost always from the right frame to the left: the way we'd read the journey if reading a map. That's the direction in which the Conestoga wagons roll, sun-auburned loaves across the prairie; and the ox carts roll; and the telegraph wire unrolls; and the rails get pounded into the earth, for the new steam engines. Sometimes the paintings show individual families; sometimes armadas of wagons. Always: west. That's where the promise is. "The frontier" is a synonym for "promise." That's where our destiny awaits us, and democracy will flourish, and what's best in us will flower and profit.

Whitman believed in the utopian spirit of this imperative, in a preordained mission "Launched o'er the prairies wide . . . / To the free skies unspent and glad and strong." It's second nature for him to write of "this land" and then breathlessly map its geography in exactly that westward movement, from "My own Manhattan with spires," through "The varied and ample land, the South and the North in the light, Ohio's shores and flashing Missouri," and onward, westward: "ever the far-spreading prairies cover'd with grass and corn." As if the Pacific lapped an American land of milk and honey.

What would he make of the railroad coolies' lashed backs, or of gold rush greed, or of all the pissy glitz and clobbered-down dreams in the strip clubs of Hollywood? Of the rattling husks of excess that we've left in our wake as litter the way that snails travel on slime? It's hard to hold to the purity of his vision.

And outer space? It is, as the original *Star Trek* says, rebooting the language of cowboy and plains homesteader, "the final frontier." As if it's taken over the westward expansion's potential

heart-thumping triumphs and potential disappointments. What
to make of our penchant for glory . . . and our ability to fuck it
up? Which one of those to bet on?

As usual I look to the poets to be my guides; as usual they remind me that it's always more complicated than purebred yin
or yang. Jon Anderson ends his poem "The Milky Way" with this
lovely evocation of galaxy-gazing in first his son's childhood,
and then his own:

> Tonight, in his play
> He captains a sleek starship
> Toward the Milky Way.

> When I was a boy, the City of
> Boston lay miles away
> Within our sight. Evenings we
> Set our chairs upon
> The lawn and talked. Few thoughts,
> A way of watching until
> Dark. Then as our small wickers
> Floated through the night
> I wished I might be taken away
> To live forever in that
> Distant city made wholly of light.

Amen, brother. However, there's also Louis Simpson's dyspep-
tic reportage from the frontier's farthest edge: "Where are you,
Walt . . . / Where is the nation you promised? . . . / The Open
Road goes to the used-car lot."

5.

The Good-bye List . . . some of its items might be the size of one
of the larger dinosaurs. The space shuttle, for example. Dead. A
dinosaur.

Some might be much smaller, though no less dearly missed for
that. A rotary dial phone. A Rolodex. What's this thing, over
here?—a box of carbon paper from 1965.

And some might be so vast—so nearly global, and so long-
standing, and so deeply dyed into the history and the mythic
tropes of our culture—that it seems they must be eternal. And
yet as I write this I can hear the wheeze, the winds-of-finality
wheeze, through the halls of the post office. Good-bye, mail
carrier's leather shoulder pouch. I won't forget you, ever, lick-
able stamp. I liked that intimacy.

Good-bye, Underwoods, Smith Coronas, Remingtons, Royals:
you were sturdy and faithful and gleamed like a mobster's sedan.

Farewell, journalism as a college major.

Privacy, adieu.

Sayonara, casual sexual pleasure without the foreboding presence of AIDS.

The Museum of Obsolescence is calling all boom boxes, penman-
ship books, cassettes, and handheld transistor radios to stand in
the Adiós Line to wait for eventual processing.

Dinosaur bones. Dinosaur bones.

The January 2012 *Discover* "note[s] the passing of the first and only reusable spaceship, the space shuttle, on July 21, 2011." There's its photo: the shuttle *Atlantis*, not pointing arrow-like and proudly toward the heavens from its launching gantry, but flat on the ground, a little ungainly, peeling, nicked, having traveled nearly 126 million miles over thirty-three flights.

"It was 39 years old. The shuttle program had been suffering for several years from a wasting loss of enthusiasm for its high price tag and untamed risks. The final cause of death was failure to find any reason to keep pouring billions of dollars into an obsolete space ferry that lacked a striking mission . . . [although it] initially embodi[ed] the dream that space travel might become routine and that we could establish an orbital beachhead for ambitious exploration of the moon and beyond."

Good-bye, exotic Martian excursions under the pas de deux of moons. We were feathered, if briefly, in the womb. That doesn't mean we were born to fly.

From David Freeman Hawke's *Nuts and Bolts of the Past:* "Any history of the machines that built America . . . must not assume that an advance on one front routinely swept through society. It is generally accepted that two Americans invented the first workable airplane. But the nation did not quickly exploit what the Wright brothers gave it. The initiative soon passed elsewhere. By 1913, Russian aircraft were bigger, French faster, German stronger. . . . The Wrights had grown middle-aged; and a native American aircraft industry had not grown with them."

Good-bye, good-bye.

6.

"Bella," they were going to name her: "beautiful." But the car broke down on their way to the natal center, and she slid—almost effortlessly, on a small wing of birth blood—into this life below a rural Massachusetts sky in which the stars seemed bent as close as apples for picking . . . and so it switched last-minute to "Stella," the name she held to in school like a prophecy, and when she was nine or ten she was *sure* that one day she'd be an astronaut, zooming among those fiery freckles.

That didn't work out. So little did. But she did become part of the mechanical crew for the shuttle—just to be near it, to be associated with it, to have handled some of its sky-eating gizmos, never failed to fill her with awe. *That* was a privilege worth living for!

Now, of course, it's all history. And somewhere inside she *does* know that, robotically, telescopically, computerly, the exploration of space will continue, just as she knows what geneticists know, and what Freud knew: there are *many* "frontiers," all of them excitingly virgin terrain; and all demanding a valorous heart and a beveled intelligence.

Still though . . . *the shuttle* . . . people in space! She made a last elegiac visit to see it—looking already like the mock-up of a tyrannosaurus skeleton in some small-town natural history museum—and then she hit the road for San Diego, to see if her reconciliation talks with Stan might go better in person than through an e-mail account.

Maybe. They'll see. The Pacific washes around her toes with a gentle indifference. Gulls. The pale wafer look of an early moon. She bends and lifts a starfish off its hold on the wet sand. Little fellow Stella riding the currents of the universe.

7.

And the man in the emergency room with a lightbulb up his ass ("And he'd packed it *deep!*").

And the woman: a golf ball up her pussy.

In the era of Vietnam my friend Alan's brother Jerry went to his army physical with strawberry jam up his rectum: he was hoping it looked like hemorrhoids. Was he crazy? Hell, the whole *war* was crazy. The nation was bipolar.

And the woman who wanted to "teach [her] son a lesson"—he'd been crying when she turned her trick in the other room—so bungee-corded that four-year-old to the trunk of her Buick and drove that way the entire three miles back from the Broadway Hotel.

And the man who was caught with his pants down, humping himself against a sun-warmed block of gypsum . . . he had a fetish for—and *only* for—gypsum, and this was his seventh offense. He was an officer in his church, a father of five, a Boy Scout troop master.

This doesn't even *begin* to approach the history of congressional shame, of corporate malfeasance, of the medical industry's fatal nincompooperies, of advertising and Facebook and Google malfeasance, of sleeper terrorist cells, of the cops on the take, of the Ponzi scheme, of the baby cereal cut with sugared sawdust.

And in May of last year Oneal Ron Morris, "a 30-year old transgendered woman," who had no medical license, nonetheless convinced "an unidentified woman who wanted a 'bigger butt' to help her get work in nightclubs" to pay him seven hundred dollars for what he said was "plastic surgery" and what turned out to be a series of "injections into her backside of a toxic mixture of Fix-a-Flat tire sealant, mineral oil and concrete." The incisions were patched up with superglue. *Concrete!* Not that you really want a thorough list of what's in lipstick.

Maybe a "sapiens" species like ours is simply never going to find a final panacea for cancer; or do without shrinks (or gods; or wars over gods); or ever take the right pure combination of breaths that will let us rise, with follow-through, to the secrets of other planets.

*

In Lukian of Samosota's *True History* (circa AD 165), a masted sailing vessel is whooshed up into the heavens by a whirlwind and carries fifty Greek athletes, in eight days, to the moon.

In Firadausi's Persian epic *Shah-Nama* (1010), four vigorous eagles bear King Kai-Kaus (still on his golden throne!) to the moon.

In Ariosto's *Orlando Furioso* (1516), the hero Astolfo commands a chariot pulled by four wingèd horses to a moon complete "with rivers, valleys, cities, towns and even castles."

In Francis Godwin's *The Man in the Moon; or, A Discourse of a Voyage Thither* (1638), the hero heads for the moon on a platform tethered to trained geese.

In Cyrano de Bergerac's novel (first English edition, 1659), a lunar journey is accompanied via vials of dew that are strapped to the traveler's body: the sun, he explains, draws dew up into the sky.

In Captain Samuel Brunt's *A Voyage to Cacklogallinia*, the lunar conveyance is an enormous basket-like palanquin borne by gigantic fowl in protective leather jackets.

And more, and others, and further. Up—the compulsion is up. By the time the *CCCP-2* reaches the moon in Vasilij Zhuralev's silent classic *Kosmischeskij rejs* (Cosmic voyage) (begun in 1930 and released in 1936), it rides on a booster rocket of thousands of years of fevered human dreaming of precisely this extraordinary venture. The great finned spaceship is so noble and assured in its aerodynamic lines—so emblematic of "thrust" and "voom" and "exploration"—the viewer can't doubt its success.

And yet in mid-November 2011, a thirteen-pound metallic ball— "a hydrazine tank from an unmanned rocket, commonly used in satellite launches"—fell near a village in Namibia; NASA's defunct Upper Atmosphere Research Satellite (6.5 tons) "plunged into the atmosphere over the Pacific Ocean"; Germany's 2.7-ton Roentgen Satellite fell into the Indian Ocean; and in January 2012 the Pacific Ocean was struck by fragments of a Russian 4.5-ton Mars probe. "Up" may be the dream, but "down" is the balancing reality.

For every direction, there is an equal and opposite direction.
For every ascending atom of aspiration, a gravitron.

Maybe even now a few vials of dew and some horse wing-feathers are washing up on a rocky New Zealand shore.

8.

At the start of *A Princess of Mars* (1912), the first of Edgar Rice Burroughs's eleven Barsoomian novels ("Barsoom" is the Martians' name for their planet), we're introduced to former Confederate army captain John Carter in the winter of 1865 as he mystically ascends from the Arizona desert (itself, of course, a landscape of red-tone sands) to the red-tone plains of what will soon become his adoptive home. "I turned my gaze from the ["Arizona moonlit landscape"] to the heavens where the myriad stars formed a gorgeous and fitting canopy for the wonders of the earthly scene. My attention was quickly riveted by a large red star *[sic]* close to the distant horizon. As I gazed upon it I felt a spell of overpowering fascination—it was Mars. . . . It seemed to call across the unthinkable void, to lure me to it. . . . My longing was beyond the power of opposition. I closed my eyes, stretched out my arms . . . and felt myself drawn with the suddenness of thought through the trackless immensity of space."

Over the course of these books he will win the hand of Dejah Thoris (always termed "the incomparable"), Princess of Helium, daughter of Tardos Mors, Jeddak of Helium; and will befriend Tars Tarkas, foremost of the swordsmen of the green (and four-armed) barbarian race of Tharks; and will battle the Priests of Omeon on the shore of their inner-world sea; and will battle the Plant Men of the Valley Dor and its River Iss, those carnivorous guards of the Holy Therns; and will commandeer the war fleet of Helium, huge troop-bearing airships powered unfailingly by the mysterious Eighth Ray.

It's the spell of this adolescent but unrefusable fantasia under which science fiction maestro Ray Bradbury falls at the age of ten, just one year after Buck Rogers enters his life: "For how can one resist walking out of a summer night to stand in the middle of one's lawn to look up at the red fire of Mars quivering in the sky and whisper: *Take me home.*"

We start in our childhood by looking to the planets for adventure, for the dilated stare of "Oh wow," and if we hold to those dreams in maturity we wind up wanting to know if there are silicates in the soil of Mars, and how the feathery runnels on its cliffs were formed and what percentage of what gas circles its poles. We want to measure its erosion, double-check its quotient of alkalis, and triple- and tetra- and penta-check for a residue hint of bacteria. That's "oh wow" also—maybe more so. And the other questions aren't far behind: What is existence? Why are we "here" at all? And who are "we"? Religious questions, only without a deity involved. That's a pretty important quest; it shouldn't be denied; and if it begins with the yearning to blast off with the Space Patrol in search of romantic dazzlements . . . well, that's as fine an entry point as any.

I live in Kansas. The state motto is *Ad astra per aspera,* "Through difficulty, to the stars." Out in the Flint Hills, where the bullying wattage of city streets can't penetrate, they still seem potent and personal enough for conversation. *Fly to me.* You can hear them, in an ear inside your ear. Clyde Tombaugh was raised on a Kansas family farm; a self-taught astronomer, "studying the heavens at night with a 9-inch reflecting telescope that he made himself," he found employment at the Lowell Observatory and in 1930 discovered what he called "Planet X"—what we call Pluto. *Be more.*

When I say that I want to fly to the moon, I mean . . . what, exactly? Not that I want to be strapped inside a tin can shot by blammo-power into the realm of zero gravity and danger. What, are you *crazy*? There's not Dramamine in the world enough to entice me.

I mean . . . I want to write a poem that's good enough to endure beyond my own bodily life; I want to work at a marriage that's finally larger and more luminous than either myself or my wife as individuals; and I want to live in a country I can be proud of, under leaders who represent me, and who fund a future that's good enough to endure beyond our own national identity. When I look above Wichita, Kansas, to the nightshine overhead, I find a language for this, beyond English.

What's "aspiration" after all, if not the worlds-engendering breath of "inspiration" turned outward, into the cosmos?

Fly to me. Be more.

9.

The ancients believed the stars were portents. Kingdoms ascended or sundered, infants healed or succumbed, according to the blinks and reconfigurations of those governing controls. A star that fell to Earth was especially an indication; soothsayers were the first deconstructionists.

So maybe the starfish she found on the sands *was* somehow predictive. Now she works as a docent in a coastal village aquarium just an hour up from where Stan lives. Their talks, so far, for the last six months, have been . . . inconclusive. Not adversarial, though, or prohibitive. So they'll see. And for now, there's real pleasure in the tanks of fish—the tiny brilliant jujubes as well as the great slow swimmers like ponderous lichen-covered rocks. After sundown, as she walks the beach, the night breeze flaps about her like an ebony cloak: it's comforting.

Besides, it's the edge of the country—she *can't* go farther. And when she looks behind . . . That one time back near Plymouth, for her mother's funeral, nothing was the same. Her high school; Joanie's always iffy marriage; that bar they used to party at after work with the three-for-one specials . . . everything grew sodden and disappeared around the time the cancer started to dissolve her mother. Even that beautiful wedding-cake-of-a-house, which *was* her childhood: first sold, then neglected, and finally razed for the upcoming mall.

She saw them on YouTube recently: *Atlantis* and *Discovery* and *Endeavor* grouped together for a final photo op. It was meant to be honorific, maybe a hundred silent people in the shadows of those majestic constructions. Although it also had the feel of three corpses laid out for the final viewing.

The beach. At night. She looks up at that black, black, black, black field and the scattered fire-wombs of our panspermia— where we came from.

Where we came from.

But there's no going back home.

SOURCES

The Adventures of Form and Content, on nearly every page, is informed by, and so indebted to, a crazy-quilt personal library of readings—from entire books like (this is only one of many examples) Mary Douglas's *Purity and Danger,* to small sidebars in an ever-branching, sloughing, accreting community of magazines and newspapers (or, often enough, to what became my notes from those sources, scribbled for a decade and a half onto the backs of receipts and on napkins, and now about as gone with the wind as Margaret Mitchell's fabular pre–Civil War Savannah). Given the length of time involved, and the untrackable flurry of sticky notes and scrawled-on bookmarks and clippings involved, some of the credit I should give to inspiring sources must remain implicit.

Of the journals that originally published these essays, three (the *Gettysburg Review,* the *Iowa Review,* the *Southern Review*) chose not to use a list of acknowledged sources. Gone, gone, gone with the wind. What follows is a combined list of acknowledged sources for one of the three essays that originally appeared in the *Georgia Review* and the essay originally published by Tavern Books. Some of my background reading, of course, even when it isn't part of the following list, is acknowledged by title and/or author within the text of the essays themselves (as one example, Judith Thurman's compelling piece on cave art, which appeared in the *New Yorker* and which threads its way through "Annals of Absence").

On a few occasions, material even within quotation marks bears small changes for the purposes of concision or rhythm (never for content). Any errors of fact or onslaughts upon sensibility?—aim brickbats at me, not at the following.

"Two Characters in Search of an Essay"
For John Keats: primarily Denise Gigante, *The Keats Brothers,* and Robert Mighall, *Keats;* with extra content from Daniel J. Boorstin, *The Discoverers;* Richard Holmes, *The Age of Wonder;* Ginger Strand, "Company Town" *(Tin House).* For Clyde Tombaugh: David H. Levy, *Clyde Tombaugh: Discoverer of Pluto;* Marcus Chown, *Solar System;* with an able assist from Richard Grossinger, *The Night Sky,* and Michael Byers's novel *Percival's Planet.* For science fiction: Isaac Asimov, *The Stars, Like Dust;* James A. Corrick, *Double Your Pleasure: ACE S.F. Doubles;* Wilson Tucker, *To the Tombaugh Station* (both magazine and book versions). Scattered factoids were gleaned from Ross King's novel *Ex-Libris* and from a clutter of clippings from issues of *Audubon, Fortean Times, National Geographic, New Scientist,* and *Smithsonian.*

"The End of Space"
Jon Anderson, *The Milky Way: Poems, 1967–1982;* Ray Bradbury, miscellaneous statements of memoir; "DiscFlix" review of *Cosmic Voyage (Filmfax,* no. 129); "In Memoriam 1972–2011" *(Discover,* Jan./Feb. 2012); "Medical Bag" and "They Fell from Outer Space" *(Fortean Times* no. 285); Richard Grossinger, *The Night Sky;* Anna Jane Grossman, *Obsolete;* David Freeman Hawke, *Nuts and Bolts of the Past;* Jon E. Lewis (ed.), *The Mammoth Book of Eye-Witness History,* "Man Lands on the Moon, 20 July 1969"; "Butt Butcher Busted in Miami" *(National Enquirer,* Dec. 12, 2011); Frederick I.

Ordway III, *Visions of Spaceflight;* Louis Simpson, *At the End of the Open Road.*

In an early book of poems I used, as an epigraph, the following quotation from Kenneth Grahame's *The Reluctant Dragon*, and it seems worth reusing here: "What the boy chiefly dabbled in was natural history and fairy tales, and he just took them as they came, in a sandwichy sort of way, without making any distinctions; and really his course of reading strikes one as rather sensible." And a speaker in Sean Russell's novel *The Compass of the Soul:* "The story you told us that night . . . the meaning was clear, the emotional truth there for anyone to hear. The facts . . . the facts should not be mistaken for truth."

The Adventures
of Form and Content

Also by Albert Goldbarth

BOOKS OF POETRY

Coprolites

Jan 31

Opticks

Keeping

A Year of Happy

Comings Back

Different Fleshes

Who Gathered and Whispered
    Behind Me

Faith

Original Light: New and
    Selected Poems, 1973–1983

Arts and Sciences

Popular Culture

Heaven and Earth: A Cosmology

The Gods

Across the Layers: Poems Old and New

Marriage, and Other Science Fiction

A Lineage of Ragpickers,
    Songpluckers, Elegiasts & Jewelers

Adventures in Ancient Egypt

Beyond

Troubled Lovers in History

Saving Lives

Combinations of the Universe

Budget Travel through Space
    and Time

The Kitchen Sink: New and
    Selected Poems, 1972–2007

To Be Read in 500 Years

Everyday People

Selfish

CHAPBOOKS

Under Cover

Curve

The Smuggler's Handbook

Ink Blood Semen

Eurekas

Goldbarth's Horoscope Almanac

Goldbarth's Book of Occult Phenomena

Collection

Delft

The Two Domains
    (Beloit Poetry Journal)

Ancient Musics

"The Burden of Modernity" and
    Other Poems (Georgia Review)

The Book

The Mailbox

The Neighbors

Photographs of the Interiors
    of Dictators' Houses
    (Kenyon Review)

Ray Palmer, Honest Half-Pint

Startling

To the Munger Station

BOOKS OF ESSAYS

A Sympathy of Souls

Great Topics of the World

Dark Waves and Light Matter

Many Circles: New and Selected Essays

Griffin

NOVEL

Pieces of Payne

The Adventures
of Form and Content

ESSAYS

Albert
Goldbarth

GRAYWOLF PRESS

Copyright © 2017 by Albert Goldbarth

This publication is made possible, in part, by the voters of Minnesota through a Minnesota State Arts Board Operating Support grant, thanks to a legislative appropriation from the arts and cultural heritage fund, and through a grant from the Wells Fargo Foundation. Significant support has also been provided by Target, the McKnight Foundation, the Amazon Literary Partnership, and other generous contributions from foundations, corporations, and individuals. To these organizations and individuals we offer our heartfelt thanks.

Published by Graywolf Press
250 Third Avenue North, Suite 600
Minneapolis, Minnesota 55401

All rights reserved.

www.graywolfpress.org

Published in the United States of America

ISBN 978-1-55597-761-0

2 4 6 8 9 7 5 3 1
First Graywolf Printing, 2017

Library of Congress Control Number: 2016938022

Cover design: Kyle G. Hunter

CONTENTS

"Kitty ['Miss Kitty,' the Dodge City saloon proprietor/ madam made famous by actress Amanda Blake over nineteen seasons of *Gunsmoke*] may have been fictional; likely, though, in later stages the role was modeled on Dora Hand, a real-life Dodge prostitute who sang in the church chorus on Sundays."

// DOUGLAS BRODE, *Shooting Stars of the Small Screen*

The Adventures
of Form and Content

Everybody's Nickname

"MAROONED ON A WORLD OF MONSTERS!"

"SHOWDOWN ON THE SUN'S LAST PLANET!"

"WAS SHE MISTRESS OF MIRACLES OR PUPPET OF
SUPER-SCIENCE?"

"BEWARE THE MASKS OF MARS!"

"BACKWARD WORLD—OR SECRET OUTPOST OF ANOTHER
GALAXY?"

These explosive bursts of words that act as ramped-up verbal
pheromones, as flirts and barkers wooing us into ever-further
sticky embrace, are the cover descriptions under (usually; sometimes over) titles of such allure, you'd think they could easily be
self-sufficient. In order: *The Forgotten Planet, World of the Master-
minds, The Green Queen, Space Station #1, Warlord of Kor.*

I suppose it's a maxim of marketing that nothing will be left
to chance. Someone believed the novel *Voodoo Planet*—check
that out: *Voodoo Planet!*—still required the extra beckoning power
of "DUEL OF THE COSMIC MAGICIANS." And so, almost all 221 of
the gaudy lilies published as "Ace science-fiction doubles" were
gilded with lovely, punchy, overly zaftig descriptions. "PRESENT
AND FUTURE CLASH IN A WORLD OF THE PAST!" You betcha.
Resistance was futile.

And then of course there was the cover art. Although a later master of the form—say, Jack Gaughan—let you know that surrealists like de Chirico and Magritte were in his experience, the world of the classic Ace covers never effervesced out of solidity into abstraction. There were no Mondrian or Rothko wannabes here. A spaceship glittered pinpoints of nebula-dazzle off its hull with the credible tonnage that Rockwell Kent would have brought to a breaching whale. That bubble helmet a spaceman wore was *real;* you could hold it, like a goldfish bowl. And the slinky, silver-saronged space sirens—whether depicted as haughtily commanding or imperiled—had a pleasurable heated heft, the way that Vargas pinup beauties did. Each weirdly spired twenty-third-century city, and every yellow electro-zap out of a raygun's futuristically coiled muzzle, encouraged your confidence and belied its own airy fancy. This was enormously effective: to have an impossible subject—hordes of eight-armed Arcturians rampaging under purple heavens—done with all of the stolid fidelity of a sitting of Frans Hals's realistic Dutch burgher-musketeers.

But, naturally, the surest inducement to part with your thirty-five cents (as opposed to the quarter for any other paperback of the day) was the very doubleness of the enterprise: two books in one, each upside down to the other, each with its independent enticing cover and title page. Two books in one! You *couldn't* say no to *Ring Around the Sun* and *Cosmic Manhunt* in a single clamoring package. (Although, if you wavered, the latter's descriptive tag would surely cinch the deal: "FROM A WONDER WORLD HIDEAWAY SHE DEFIED THE CODE OF SPACE!")

But why am I using past tense? They're in front of me as I'm writing this, on a drugstore spinner rack I've purchased especially to display—to daily live with—my collection. Here's the intergalactic beauty of *Cosmic Manhunt* herself, although a touch more like a carnival side-tent hootchie-koo dancer than

you'd think the far-advanced techno-world of tomorrow might permit. And here's the *Rocket to Limbo*—so full of zoom! And here's the ponderous, wrinkled, eye-tentacled, seaweed-headed, lobster-clawed green alien who, in 1960, when I was twelve and thirty-five cents was a treasure (and I was aburst with dreams, with vague shapes of Adventure and Accomplishment and Ava Edelman sitting across the aisle in Astronomy), successfully encouraged my first-ever retail paperback purchase (outside of schoolroom orders): *Bow Down to Nul* by Brian W. Aldiss (the tag line, "WHEN MONSTERS RULE"; the cover, Ed Emshwiller art). Its mate: *The Dark Destroyers.*

The colorful paperback-cover bluster and showy iconography that some of us would call "tawdry" or "lurid" simply reclaim their heritage from predecessor pulp fiction magazines. Enter Aaron A. Wyn, sharp businessman and founder in 1928 of the Ace line of pulp magazines—*Secret Agent X, Ten Detective Aces, Eerie Stories**—"some of the livelier second-rung pulps in the golden age," as Lee Server puts it in *Over My Dead Body,* his history of that industry. In 1940 Wyn entered the burgeoning comic book field with *Sure-Fire Comics,* followed by an array of genre hopefuls: *Super Mystery, Love Experiences, War Heroes, Men Against Crime, Hap Hazard, Indian Braves.* They were successful enough, but by the 1950s Wyn could sense the winds of readership beginning to blow in a new direction, and once again he yielded to those currents; in 1952 he launched a paperback line, Ace Books, retaining that aegis from twenty-four years in the fields of high-acid-content paper.

Wyn's associate Walter Zacharius first suggested the gimmick

---

*Eerie Stories has been described by pop culture maven Bud Plant as "one of many 1930s pulps too hot for most newsstands." Titles from a typical issue: "The Soul-Scorcher's Lair" and "Virgins of the Stone Death."

of doubling up books in a single binding, topsy-turvying them in the now familiar format, and Wyn then hired Donald A. Wollheim to edit this new "Ace Doubles" series. (Some were to be crime and western books but, as time went on, the series became increasingly outer-spaced.) A number of tumblers were ready to click into place, with Wollheim the first of them.

Born to be a hobnobbing fan and soon after that a professional, Wollheim was, at twenty-three in 1937, forming science fiction's earliest amateur press association, distributing (to its fifty members) those hectographed magazines of fantasy orientation that driven enthusiasts cranked out ("cranked out" literally) in a circulation of twenty to thirty-five. In 1943 he was connected enough to edit what's normally credited as the first mass-market paperback anthology of science fiction stories, *The Pocket Book of Science Fiction* (for Pocket Books, a major player), having already cut his editorial teeth on the pulp science fiction magazines *Stirring Science Stories* and *Cosmic Stories*—which, says sci-fi historian James Gunn, "had an editorial budget of exactly nothing, but nevertheless lasted four and three issues respectively."* Wollheim also wrote *The Universe Makers* (Harper and Row, 1971), a sturdy history of science fiction; indeed, in the published photographs of him that I have, he *looks like* a historian out of central casting, bespectacled and slightly turtley-owlish. Avidity, expertise, the ability to generate product out of nonexistent cash flow: he was the man for A. A. Wyn!

Now . . . enter Allen Ginsberg.

---

*In the March 1941 *Cosmic Stories:* A tagline, "KELLOGG'S TIME EXPLORERS WERE TRAPPED IN A JUNGLE OF MAN-HUNTING MACHINES!" A story, "The Martians Are Coming!" An ad for the Remington Portable Noiseless Typewriter *and desk* "for as little as 10¢ a day," an ad for "Sex Secrets of Love and Marriage Daringly Revealed!" (And another story, "The Man from the Future," by one Donald A. Wollheim, billed as the "Author of 'Planet of Illusion.'")

In 1956 the mad young hipster Carl Solomon (Lee Server: "a high-strung screwup and devotee of Antonin Artaud") would enter the annals of literary history as the dedicatee of Ginsberg's seminal anthem *Howl*. They'd met in 1949 in the New York State Psychiatric Institute. Ginsberg was there under false (well, semi-false) pretenses. Nabbed by the cops for joyriding in the company of some burglar pals (along with their boodle of stolen dresses), and finding his quickly concocted alibi unaccepted (a newspaper headline laconically noted, "Boy Joins Gang to Get 'Research' for Story"), he'd pleaded insanity as preferable to jail. Here he was now, in the nuthouse.

Solomon, though, was a version of the real-deal certifiable nut outsider, and was undergoing shock treatments, the results of which were amnesia and convulsions. This accidental friendship of theirs provided the neophyte poet with material from Solomon—long-winded diatribe-stories of his adventures ("who talked continuously seventy hours from park to pad to bar to Bellevue to museum to the Brooklyn Bridge . . .")—that seven years later would fuel the mid-twentieth-century's most explosive American poem.

But *three* years after their seraphic-demonic talkfests in the mental institution, Carl Solomon would be making the attempt to reenter everyday straight life, as symbolized mainly by his taking on a job, an "acquiring editor's position" at the offices of his uncle—the publisher A. A. Wyn. At this same moment Ginsberg had also taken on a job, more unofficially, acting as literary agent for some of his wanderlust-afflicted writer friends. And so one day in 1952 finds Ginsberg on West Forty-Seventh Street, at Ace Books, trying to peddle two manuscripts.

Solomon is worried that his endorsement of this edgy stuff might only reconfirm his family's dubious opinion of his sanity. On the other hand, Ginsberg's zeal is infectious, and the writing—street smart and visceral—is abristle with compelling

hooks . . . and, to Ginsberg's delight and Solomon's credit, a couple of low three-figure offers eventually are extended.

One of these books—the one with its manuscript type-written on a roll of uncut Teletype paper—is never to be published by Ace. Solomon requested substantial rewrites, and the author—impatient, egotistical, chafing under the criticism—entered into a series of rancorous shouting bouts with his editor, one time threatening to break Solomon's glasses, and finally withdrew his wunderkind tome from the paper empire of A. A. Wyn.

And thus was Kerouac's *On the Road,* that ur-text of Beat literature, only a tantrum away from joining the ranks of *Android Avenger; Earthman, Go Home!; The Stars Are Ours!;* and *Slavers of Space.*

And thus did Ginsberg's other (and somewhat more standardly written) offering join the list of Ace Doubles as D-15: *Junkie,* by the pseudonymous William Lee, paired up (or "69d," as Ginsberg described it) with Maurice Helbrant's *Narcotic Agent.* Today that thirty-five-cent book—"William Lee," of course, was William Burroughs—can be valued at over a thousand-fold (if near mint) in a vintage paperback auction. Some might want it as well for the showily shadowy dames-and-needles-and-handcuffs cover by genre artist Al Rossi.

Not that *Junkie* ever sold astoundingly well, and soon thereafter Ginsberg lost his "in" at Ace—his dreams of foisting types like Jean Genet and Neal Cassady on a mass-market readership dissipated in tandem with the stability of Solomon, who shortly began to unravel under the pressures of an editor's day.

And thus we leave him, that difficult man, in only four more years to be memorialized by *Howl* ("ah, Carl . . . now you're really in the total animal soup of time") but right now scampering crazily "through traffic on Eighth Avenue," says Lee Server, "screaming and throwing his suitcase and shoes at passing vehicles."

And yet we *don't* leave him. We can never leave him, or at least we can't leave what he comes to represent, or *it* won't leave us. We can't shake the workaday man in the suit and tie, the pick-up-the-kids-and-the-groceries mom, who turn around and— voilà!—the gibbering, capering, levitating, gods-conversing, screw-you, fuck-me, soaring-through-the-risen-cream-of-the-origin-of-the-universe otherself is on display to the world. Nor can we free ourselves from the opposite knowledge: inside the incarcerated and the hopeless, the beyond-the-fringe and the up-for-grabs, is a man who longs to mow his lawn to the neighborhood association code and a woman who's fossicking the checkbook at the end of her day. What thin spit and ephemeral synaptic flimmer bind these halves together!

And we *are* compounded of halves. The heart is our great bicameral house. Our cells are the glorious ringing echo of the duet between a Y chromosome and an X. We're each a working system of an impossibillion positive and negative specter-charges in a delicate ritual balance, and in this of course we're the infrastructure of even larger systems that began at the Bang and function the same. All of our myths almost uniformly reflect this: male/female; Fire Bringer/Bearer of Waters; mind/matter; angel/ape-thing lurking in the dark—ineradicably. Religious precept understands (and fears) how the philanderer is the unspoken twin of the penitent. Popular fiction understands—all of those pulp extravaganzas: Zorro! The Spider! The Whisperer!— how a superhero somehow consists of the same collection of molecules as his more mundane identity.

Here are two stories out of the midsized Midwest city in which I live.

The first is one of those heart-tug pieces my local paper so loves to dote over. In May 1997, Ray Robinson Jr., age eleven, was written up as "mayor for the day." A formerly troublesome

(and, one can tell, "disadvantaged") student at College Hill Elementary School, the now fifth-grader had "turned himself around" and "even started helping . . . work with a troubled first-grader."

When Robinson told his teacher Nancy Hughey that current mayor Bob Knight "was his hero" ("I didn't think he was aware [we] *had* a mayor," said Hughey), word escaped, and in a snap of media time it was photo-op heaven: "Knight had the boy come to City Hall [and] sit in the mayor's seat in the council chambers." In the photograph that finally ran, we see a beaming black child (his smile could warm its way through permafrost) with his arms around the waist of a benevolently smiling middle-aged white politico guy, who hugs him back. It's the paradigmatic 1997 feel-good shot.

"Ray is very focused these days about his goals and what he wants," Hughey said. "Sometimes he slips and says 'If I am mayor . . .' then immediately corrects himself, saying, 'When I am mayor . . .' And then, 'I want to be somebody when I grow up.'"

The second story is also about a grade school student who once assumed a short-term political office: Chelsea Brooks, landslide-elected vice president of the "fifth-grade project to study how government works." "She took her job very seriously," said her classroom teacher. "Leadership and charisma were everyday traits for Chelsea." The praises continue: "very bright, confident," "loyal," "such an amazing girl," "funny, smiling," "so much promise." You can start to see all this in the photo the paper keeps using: another smile that beams—from out of the usual daily murk of war and inflation and global warming—like a lighthouse.

A few days after Chelsea's eighth-grade graduation, on June 15, 2006, her body was found by workers, strangled to

death and nine months pregnant, in a shallow grave by a wheat field off a rutted dirt road in Butler County. She had planned "to go to college." She was going to name the baby Alexa Lynn.

Her murder was contracted out, the state claims, by the father—who had been pressuring her to keep his identity secret, afraid he'd otherwise wind up in jail on charges of statutory rape. She was crazy about him, her friends say; she'd do anything for him. "'I love him to death,'" her friend Kali quotes Chelsea as saying. Presumably his pressure was starting to fail, and a more secure measure occurred to him. On the night of June 9 Chelsea left the Skate South skate park on MacArthur near Hydraulic "to see," she told her friends, "the father of [my] baby." The next time anyone saw her, she was a corpse.

In one accompanying photograph two classmates of Chelsea's hold each other and weep—a common shot by now, "the Columbine pose," I call it. Their faces are buried in one another's grief. In another photograph—paired with hers, as she would have paired up pictures of them on the inside of her locker—is the father, staring sullenly. He's charged with capital murder, aggravated kidnapping, and two counts of rape "for allegedly having sex with Chelsea before her 14th birthday." (Chelsea's mother claims, "In 2004 he was [also] caught in a park with [another] 14-year-old girl.") His face is dazed and scared and insolent and hardly recognizable at all as that of Elgin "Ray-Ray" Robinson, nine years after his one day as guest mayor.

An extreme example, for sure, but which of us *isn't* two people, nestled together? Or wrestled. "My father was a political radical," Betsy Wollheim writes in a reminiscence, "but he was conservative personally." And she says, "Many people loved him." And she adds, "Many people feared him."

It seems that Donald A. Wollheim had it right. Everyone's backed by a second narrative. Everybody's nickname is Ace.

In some of the doubles the halves are conjoined with an easy inevitability. D-295, for instance: two Jack Vance novels seamed together, both of them barnstorming, gutsy, other-galactic tours (*Slaves of the Klau* and *Big Planet*) done in an early stage of his highly distinctive style. Or later, D-403: *The Pirates of Zan* and *The Mutant Weapon*, both by Murray Leinster.

Other duos are more discrepant: a story of time travel (ancient Rome) matched with a look at some twenty-fourth-century outpost on Mars. And how, among all the swashbuckler/gung-ho/wondrous interplanetary voyaging of so many of these titles, to find a fit partner for one of Philip K. Dick's increasingly dyspeptic, dour, and psychopharmacologically inspired views of "tomorrow"?

All of this halving and doubling reaches a lovely critical mass on the cover (I'd guess it's by Robert Schultz, although it's uncredited) of Andre Norton's *The Crossroads of Time* ("A CHASE THROUGH ALTERNATE WORLDS"). Its central image is of a man staring out at us, full-front. The face's left-hand side we clearly read as a portrait of a soldier of the future (he wears a soldier-of-the-future helmet); in back, a futuristic city skyline: plump cigar-silhouetted rocket ship and buildings that muscle upward with flanges and doohickey walkways bespeaking a leap of centuries. The right-side face is a portrait of a twentieth-century man (the book appeared in 1956—the year of *Howl*'s publication); in back, a mid-twentieth-century downtown cityscape, with airplane and an Empire-State-Building building lifting out of the foggy streets. They merge: they make a single face. So tell me, is the invisible vertical line between the two a glitch?—or a bridging? Keep in mind that the novel itself is half of D-164 and so is backed by (at the same time, is the back of) *Mankind on the Run* (Gordon R. Dickson). Keep in mind that the prolific Andre Norton ("author of over one hundred novels") is a woman—she also published as Andrew North. (And for whoever finally pro-

duces Mary Alice Norton's biography: I recommend you utilize
the cover of *The Crossroads of Time* as a template, with a female-
male division-and-blend laid over the original.)

The more I look at this book in the days of my writing this
essay, the more the rest of the world conforms. A man named
John Rybicki has asked if I'll supply a blurb for his first collection of poems; on one page I find:

> "You're living two lives now," I tell him rolling out
> of Detroit in my truck . . .

> "You slip your arms out of a fur coat made of bricks.
> And when we get back home, trade it

> for a fur coat made of cornfields."

There you have it. I open an issue of *Fortean Times,* that monthly
compilation of "unusual phenomena," and I find that Jessica
Sandy Booth attempted "to hire a hitman to kill four men and
steal a block of cocaine she had seen in their house in Memphis."
The "cocaine" "turned out to be Mexican queso fresco cheese,"
the "hitman" was an undercover cop. They make a single
face—"A CHASE THROUGH ALTERNATE WORLDS" indeed.

As if a map of our own bilateral neocortex weren't enough to
conjure up that cover of Andre Norton's book as a hovering tute-
lary spirit. The brain is butterflied into its left-right hemispheres:
sometimes, in a certain aspect, they work with a uniform will; at
other times, these wings have seemingly landed here, each from
a different world, and become hinged arbitrarily.

If you snip and peel back the dura, the thin but leathery
membrane-shield over the brain, then there they are: the mirror-
image mazes where our thought exists and where our commands to ourselves are created. Carl Sagan refers to them as

"two semi-independent brains." But we do—and really it's most proper to—consider them parts of a single thing, the one "grey vault of Heaven," as Shakespeare puts it in *Henry IV, Part II.*

Even so, there are maladies so unfortunate that a few of us undergo hemispherectomies (1923 was the first, by a Baltimore neurosurgeon). The patients usually do surprisingly well. Although, as Christine Kenneally says, "it is generally thought that language is situated in the left half of the brain," it turns out all left-lobe hemispherectomees still talk. "Many children who have had [the operation] are in high school, and one, a college student, is on the dean's list."

Still, grievous aversion to any removal of our symmetries is understandably woven throughout the fabric of us. At the same time that my local paper is covering Chelsea Brooks's murder, it's covering the trial of the (now-convicted) murderer of county sheriff's deputy Kurt Ford. Testifying in court was twin sister Karla Ford: "The other half of me is gone."

In the earliest days of the hemispherectomy process, at the conclusion of it, when one of the Gemini lobes was gone and the suddenly empty space called out for filling, "they would put all kinds of things in the cranial cavity—one surgeon used sterile Ping-Pong balls." I *like* the image of stuffing the skull with those small light spheres that, after all, were made exactly to travel back and forth across the halves of a whole.

First on the statistical side. Then on the creative side. Speech over here. Motor skills there. Potayto. Potahto. Tomayto. Tomahto.

Somehow we bring it all off. I'm reminded of Ginsberg's bon mot, "69d." In a cheezoid porn mag I have is a photographic sequence of a couple performing exactly that. In the final scene, they're satiated and resting: not engaged in sexual pleasure any longer, but still in that same position: relaxed now into a circle—*the* circle—of difference-and-similarity.

She said her name was Gaea now.

And so it made a kind of "poetic sense" that I met her in what they termed an "Earth Sciences" course.

I couldn't pull my gaze away. If she *were* the earth, then she had two orbiting satellites: my eyes.

She was the standard "coed hippie chick" of the era—this was 1968—but given the lower-middle-class neighborhood of my upbringing, she was the sweep of a fresh, invigorating breeze, with her ass-length unpermed hair, her genuine and unadorned smile, her tiny massage-me toes in their sensible sandals. I would have followed her to set up a treehouse residence at the heart of any leech-infested rain forest of her choosing, she was so . . . "different" is the only way I could say it, although my sappiest poems of that year attempted an eloquence on her behalf, with "halcyon" and "alabaster" and "beauteous" and—a loosely Ginsbergian influence—"heart-electricity-sylph."

"Different," but . . . familiar too, the way she sat across from me in class. Like . . . she was Ava, I realized. Ava Edelman. Wow. From seventh grade. And look at how she'd willfully metamorphosed from that shallow, eye-shadowed, cashmered girl. The strength to which I attributed that transformation only further ratcheted up my infatuation. Stratosphere-level. Ionosphere-level. There was no stopping my lust-and-googoo trajectory up from the launchpad.

She had taken her current name, she said, to match her "current being": she was "an advocate of our mother planet." Okay by me. Whatever.

And she was flattered I'd remembered her—flattered, I think, that out of all the men who gathered around the dancing slopes below the showcase scoop of her peasant blouse and the cling of the African-pattern skirt to her hips, I was the only one who knew enough to appreciatively chart the arc of her evolution. One day

she got out the old class notes from Astronomy, and the textbook, and we reminisced. And then we carnally tussled.

She was so . . . "pure." She was so pure and "free"—"like the animals in nature." She was sexy, but pure, if pure is a way of saying no to makeup and choosing a bicycle over "fossil fuels." And under the lure of the musks of her body, I wanted to be pure too. I think she enjoyed, in her own way, having an acolyte, a trainee. This was a time when my friend Mitch became a Marxist mainly to gain the affections of Frances Shteck and spent three nights in the city jail martyring himself (in vain, it turned out) to that cause. And Darcy—she left an A average and invitations from seven East Coast graduate schools in favor of leather leashes and a man whose biker name was Seven Sins. So it didn't seem odd to me to mold myself toward Gaea's needs. I doubt I even knew that I was doing it.

She liked that I was "gentle." Fine: I emphasized my gentleness. It was like natural selection. And her daily code *was* admirable. "No" to preservatives. "No" to meat foods. "No" to artificial soup-to-nuts. Ah, but the "yes" she'd murmur at night, when her roommates had blessedly left us alone for an hour. . . . For that, I'd have gouged the fillings out of my teeth—such manmade obscenities!

You can tell, I'm sure, where this is leading. Before we reached that point, however, we *did* share wonderful times. They didn't need to be outwardly major moments—a European tour, a backstage pass. The smallest event could feel as if it let extra worlds into this one: reading her a passage out of Thoreau while she reclined in the bath, the candlelight bringing his sure-grip words and her slippery shoulder into an alliance. And I came to see myself as I believed *she* saw me: it wasn't shyness, it was tenderness. I was a kind of sachem of tenderness.

The falling apart was total cliché. It happened out of town—down at the beach, in fact—at a Green-Think Weekend

Getaway. She got away, all right. Around seven o'clock on that Saturday night I turned a corner of heaped-up brush and abandoned jetty piles, and there she was with another man, a specialist on recycling waste into energy sources. I'm telling you, *with* another man. Her neon fuchsia bikini bottom was floating out on the blue of the bay as loud as a four-car pileup.

So we had it out in the room that night—anger, guilt, defensiveness, and all of the other carrion birds. I called her a slut. She'd *told* me she was "free," she hadn't *lied* to me, wasn't I *listening?* And then I slapped her. Yes, that's what Mr. Gentle did in his pig-blind rage. I must have thought it didn't come *close* to the hurt that she'd dealt me. You want to be "free," huh? "Like an animal," Miss Purity? Go watch a nature movie. (And then my hand struck.) There! *That's* how animals act.

We never completely recovered from that confrontation, although some do. The trouble, as you can see, was not her betrayal of me with Victor Vegan, nor was it my one-time violent swipe. The real trouble was the way we'd seen each other all along—as singular things that meant one message only. Yes, but we each had another side too, like anyone. That shouldn't have been surprising. Still, we were young and we were inflexible, and whatever those "other sides" of us were, they hadn't fit the dynamic as we'd been living it. The following morning I sulked off by myself and had a triple bacon cheeseburger: breakfast. It was *goooood.*

We never completely recovered, but twice that year we made an attempt. I'm thinking right now of a night with wine and slightly drunken petting, over at her apartment. She goes to bed and leaves me restlessly awake still, at her work desk. I can look through the door and watch the moon's long intimacy with that shoulder I used to suds.

And I idly page through her papers. There, the old textbook: Astronomy. A picture of the earth from space, exactly one-half

in the full touch of the sun and exactly one-half in shadow. Not a single thing at all.

I look at that earth, through time and wine and a thousand compounded emotions, and I look until there are many earths, or anyway many planets, zooming amazingly through the skies of those books I used to read for just thirty-five cents. In one, the aliens clobbered us. In another, we emerged triumphant. Whoever the "aliens" were by then—and, of course, whoever "we" were.

Roman Erotic Poetry

This seems to be the summer of com-, recom-, and uncombining.

Once a week I do (or "undergo," if she's steaming away her angst at some ferocious power speed) a walk around (and around and around) Hill Park with Martha. Arthur's just moved out of the house this month, supposedly to "reconnect with himself" and reconsider the marriage. "Albert, today I think"— but *really* what she means is "this five minutes I think," and then she pre-rejects it—"or maybe not." I've been alongside Orthodox rabbis studying the yolks of eggs in search of the tell-tale pinpoint of blood that would render the meal unfit for a kosher plate, I've seen crew techies fussily inspect the engines of film set stuntmobiles before a dangerous chase . . . but *nobody* comes close to the atoms-parsing exactitude of Martha dissecting her marriage's strife. "He *might* be thinking . . ." Tolkien, even, couldn't explore so many finely realized imaginary worlds.

And then again there's Sweet and Danny. Can't *they* see it? Everyone else can see it. Every day he passes her desk, and she passes his desk, and they pass by "chance" in the mailroom, and the building—all ten stories of it—seems to realign itself in generous accord to the complicated physics of human attraction. *Say something* already, one of you. Go on, do it! That nonchalance is sheerer than the negligee on the cover of the

current Frederick's catalog, and the breathy yearnings under it are all too clear. Look, we're rooting for you, but help us out! There are bets on this. They circle closer, then break away. Then circle again: a little tighter in, this time. Tomorrow? Look at her goo-blue, Lake-of-the-Ozarks eyes! His chin with its first goatee! What are the odds being quoted this afternoon by the Sweet and Danny pundits for tomorrow?

But tomorrow I'm also having lunch with Ed, whose life has been hurtfully empty of anyone, or any possibility, for three or four years. And then I'm supposed to drop by Yancy's: you know, Yancy, who spent an hour randily experimenting with Gal Pal 3 as Gal Pal 5 was lazily driving around the block, awaiting her turn for his Buddha talk and beautifully broken-in prizefighter face.

This seems to be the summer, all right.

And that's not even mentioning Mister J and George, my two gay friends who have been a stable couple for as long as I've lived in this city. "Stable . . . but gay. The unwanted ten percent." (And Mister J chips in, "In *this* city? Maybe about, oh, zero-point-five.") "So even the best of days, there's always this sense of an outside chemistry that intrudes. A joke, a look. And it could even be a well-intentioned look, but it's *always there*." And an image from Mister J: "It's like we're just two cars with their hoods up, side by side, attempting to jump each other's engines. See? But there's traffic all around: the other ninety percent. Gawking, honking, offering advice. It makes it more tough to get charged."

I'm telling you now what I hope to do in the sections that follow: simply show how friends of mine have often inspired long thought on the subject of sexual pairing; how that one thought organized everything else I considered and did in the summer of the year 2003.

"Long thought . . . ," "organized . . ."—it sounds so arid and geometric. But these are my friends. The "thought" is salted, from out of their eyes and night sweats. And the "organization" is their continuous leaving and finding and missing and entering one another: lines that extend out into the world from a starting point in our DNA.

Fifty-six, in the standard editions.

That well-known and knowingly scurrilous poem of Catullus's, in which he comes across a young man "jerking off." The youth is (1) a slave in the house of Lesbia (a lover of Catullus's, who was known for her bedroom appetites) and (2) we assume, her on-call sex toy, currently supping on Lesbia's favors with a frequency that Catullus himself can only frustratingly dream of (in the Oxford translation by Guy Lee, "slave" is more winkingly rendered as "boy pet"). What Catullus does at this opportune conjunction is approach from the rear and "bang him with my hard"—thus simultaneously enjoying a serendipitous homoerotic quickie *and,* through this very literal fucking, metaphorically "fucking over" his all-too-promiscuous ladylove. "A funny thing," he calls it, "worth chuckling over."

You'd need to be quite a prig not to see the humor involved—much of it from the way form is wedded to function here. Just as the agendaless sexual lark and the agenda-ridden act of petty vengeance are a tidily compacted act, seemingly over in one swift jab (which is why, perhaps, the David Mulroy version opts for "spear" instead of "hard"), the poem itself is correspondingly only seven lines from setup to conclusion. It bears the lightning smack of a comically good vaudevillian half-a-minute.

But thinking about it afterward is liable to be discomforting. For the ethically fastidious, there's the callous yoking of sex and spite. Beyond that there's the question of how welcome is the speaker's attention. Rape?—could we credibly say this is rape? But the tone is so high-spirited! And the implication is that this horny, self-pleasuring boy may be surprised by Catullus's entry, yet not distressed. And *could* he even be surprised? The nearing, step by step; the lusty raising of the garment's hem; the business of fleshly adjustment . . . surely the boy could have skipped away easily enough *sometime* during all of that? Although . . . what *are* the rights of a slave in ancient Rome? Of

course, he isn't *Catullus's* slave in the first place. . . . So much is lost in a cross-millennial and bilingual fog. My two-book selection of variant Catullus translations attests to the slipperiness of certainty, "hard" and "spear" as just one instance. Another: "jerking off" in Guy Lee's edition is given as "wanking" in Mulroy. However, even if we could prove it was consensual and nothing but a bright, midday caprice for its participants amid the hurly-burly of Rome in AD 56 (or thereabouts), as one was leisurely making his way on behalf of his owner to the market, and one was off to the baths . . . you know that the very idea of same-sex union is abhorrent to many (to you? to that guy over there? to me?). As Mister J once said, "It doesn't matter how decent George and I might be as individuals. As a couple, we give 'em the willies."

So: what is and what isn't a proper coupling? We could say that the definition of those two states *is* what a culture exists for. It's not proper for a mortal to mate with a god (and still, it's *possible* in ancient Greece: when the great swan covers Leda and she rises to meet that otherworldly wingbeat, she looks wildly fletched, from head to toe). Nor should the gods disport among *themselves,* if codified prohibitions exist. In Ovid, when Venus seduces Mars (adulterously: she's married to Vulcan), the poet passes unmediatable censure: "It was wrong." *And* consequential: "Then Vulcan's mind went dark. He dropped his work and at once began crafting revenge." So it turns out even the Olympians are assumed to be delimited in their choices! (It's like discovering that the God of the Judeo-Christian bibles, for all of his omnipotent zap, is constrained to work his miracles through the unyielding laws of college physics: mesoscale convection vortices, crystal lattice alignment, tectonic slippage.)

To marry across the lines of caste in traditional Indian culture is strenuously forbidden; a Brahmin-Nayar pair would be as grotesque as some 1950s monstrosity out of a Hollywood

one-week wonder: a lizard-ape or a gorilla-panther rampaging about in its ill-fitted halves. In Shakespeare too: between the tangled worlds of Montague and Capulet, a chasm intervenes, so deep and wide across that the bodies of both sides' children will plummet helplessly into its shadows and be broken on the rocks at the bottom. Ask the pope in 1633 if Galileo has permission to conduct the marriage of Earth and sky: the answer is no; the answer is that *some* possible combinations of human material and human spirit are always going to be on the "forbidden" list, in the interests of keeping ever intact the *sanctioned* combinations of a culture; the answer is simply that, to kill his vision, this fine old man with the astronomical truth in his head will be threatened, very persuasively, with torture (say, "correction") in the dungeons of the Inquisition. Some marriages are so dangerous, the fright they create in the cultural authority is *immediately* translated into loathing, before the fear can be consciously registered.

And high among these is homosexual marriage. What else so direly lays siege to mainstream gender roles in the majority population and implicitly undermines its basic structural unit, the hetero nuclear family? In the first code of laws for Plymouth Colony in 1636, "sodomy" and "buggery" (along with murder and "solemn compaction with the devil by way of witchcraft") take their place on a list of "capital offenses liable to death." Most often, "buggery" was what we'd term bestiality. In 1642 Love Brewster's seventeen-year-old servant Thomas Granger was hanged on the gallows for committing this pollution with (in William Bradford's account) "a mare, a cow, two goats, five sheep, two calves and a turkey," and before the noose was snugged around that young man's neck, "first the mare and then the cow and the rest of the lesser cattle were killed before his face, according to the law, Leviticus xx.15" (for this is no longer a God who appears to his supplicants aroused, aflame, in the

guise of a swan or a heifer). "And the cattle were all cast into a great and large pit that was digged of purpose for them, and no use made of any part of them." Even the flinty Bradford finds the outcome "very sad."

And in 1641 in Puritan Massachusetts Bay Colony, a servant "of twenty or under" was charged with sodomy and duly hanged. If that's the standard, then John Alexander was lucky—in 1637 he appeared before the court with Thomas Roberts, the both of them "found guilty of lewd behavior and unclean carriage one with another, and often spending their seed one upon another." For this "the said John Alexander was therefore censured by the Court to be severely whipped, and burnt in the shoulder with a hot iron, and to be perpetually banished from the government of New Plymouth." Because such heathenish adjoinment is an affront in the eyes of the Lord, and is of a foulness in the nostrils of Our Maker, and is an abomination for which the Afterlife awaits for ever and aye with an eternal torment of flames and the stench of brimstone.

Although the truth is—for me this week, this summer—it's Martha and Arthur who seem to be schlepping their lives through the ravenous fires of hell.

Or Marthur and Artha, as some of us had taken to saying, they always seemed *so right* for each other, so in-blended.

"*Now,* though . . . I don't know. We'll have to wait and see." Martha's voice somehow imparts to even these empty words a gravid expectation.

Her hair is a burgundy shade of auburn, descending in great cascades on either side: it frames her face like opened theater drapes. This is appropriate enough, since these days Martha's conversation appears in her face with all of the immanence, the up-close physicality, of puppets acting out the rapidly alternating highs and lows of this difficult time.

"He said he'd call this morning, but he didn't. Should I call *him?* I mean, would that be intrusive?" Before I can answer— "Or maybe he'd see that I cared, if I called. Unless he purposely didn't call to test me. Or maybe . . ." This is a woman who, a couple of months ago, would fancifully wonder if the universe was infrastructured, "from even before our species evolved," according to laws of beauty, "but even supposing the answer is yes, would it be a sort of beauty we'd recognize," and was it even possible (although horrible) that "our suffering is part of a larger, inhuman beauty that *uses us* as factors in its equations," arguing all of this with deft allusion to Keats, to the choreography of Twyla Tharp, to Greek myths. Now we huff our way through Hill Park incessantly testing the edges of Arthur-this and Arthur-that, a finite deck of Arthur cards with infinite architectural potential, and what-does-Albert-think?

The changing Hill Park prospect sometimes suns her face and then, just seconds after that, tree-shadows it—like her hopes and her fears in their puppetry show. And Albert wishes, *dearly* wishes, he knew what he thought, but he doesn't, and what he *suspects,* in his gut, is a slow-building bolus of dismal news.

In a kindly intended review of one of my books, St. Louis poet Richard Newman said, "The author comments throughout

on his characters' heartbreak, discussing our culture's failed marriages with the experience of a marriage counselor [and now my favorite part:] without the psychobabble." Ah, yes. If only friends *were* characters whose lives abide by authorly rules of beauty and whose suffering could, at the very least, be explained away in those acceptable terms. But I'm at a loss for advice, now, here, in the park, as the light and the branches deal out the scenery of our friendship.

We pass a few kids playing. "Albert . . . is there a helium balloon that's going to lift me out of this quicksand?" Who would have thought the classically minded Martha G. would one day be talking to me in images from a cliché Walgreens Valentine card? Who would have thought that Arthur's emphatically ink-black hair would one day leave the stylist's in a ring of yellow spikiness, so looking as if his head were on fire, as if he couldn't think clearly until some mental baggage—call it the "old life," maybe the old life including Martha herself—had been surrounded and burned away?

And who'd have predicted seven years ago when they first arrived, to open a small art gallery (that specialized in installation pieces), Off the Wall—a gracious, urbane, and completely in-sync young couple—that they would be so frayed on a future day? I remember the night when Nettie found some of us having a drink at the Tin Cup, sat down, ordered a first wheat beer, and said, "Wow. I just went down to the gallery, it was closed, but I looked through the window in back . . ." *Yeah? And?* "Well, they were there, sure enough. From now on, I'm calling it On the Floor."

And really: *isn't it* crazy that these two joined halves have come undone? We have reason now to believe that there was effective, and even commonly ho-hum, mating between Neanderthals and those Pleistocene people the paleoarchaeologists are wont to call "anatomically modern humans"—us. Across that amazing

genetic and physiological divide . . . and out of what had to have been the obvious species-species suspicions and competition for game . . . one specimen, "Lagar Velho 1, from 25,000 years ago, bears a combination of Neanderthal and modern human traits that could have resulted from only extensive interbreeding"—*and my friends from the same undergraduate college, Martha and Arthur, can't maintain a cohesive, functioning unit?* "In a single late-twentieth-century decade, veterinarians learned how to use the uterus of one species to carry the embryo of another"—*and Martha and Arthur, who vote the same way, and dance the same way, and rumor has it like the same position for intercourse, can't bond in a lasting polymer?* The "Feejee Mermaid" that Barnum started successfully displaying in 1842 (to a profit of almost a thousand dollars a week) . . . although "the upper half was a monkey and the lower half a fish," its anonymous Japanese village fisherman originator worked with elfin nimbleness of such an undetectable degree that several university naturalists and a slew of newspaper editors proclaimed it upon examination a single, supple creature of the sea—*and Martha and Arthur are incapable of stitching themselves back together? Can't they just kiss and make up?*

I'm thinking of Brancusi's *The Kiss,* that brick of stone so minimally but eloquently yinned and yanged. But people aren't stone, and an unscentable though real human musth can drive us wild at times; it simmers inside and presses against the forehead from behind, and then invisible but undeniable psychological chancres open all over our skin and fill us with needs for which there may not be therapy terms yet. The Neanderthals surely knew this, whatever "knowing" meant to them, and the knowledge hasn't changed over millennia; it goes back to the battle that was fought out in the caves, between our earthy, remnant brain stem and the upward aspirations of our overlayering neocortex: *it isn't easy, this being a hominid.* So, no, I *can't* say if

Martha and Arthur are going to reinstate themselves . . . and a recent visit to Arthur's, I can tell you, *doesn't* leave me aglow with hope.

I don't want to cast him as the villain in this. He has his own Arthury versions of things, as worked out on his side of the gulf, and they have their own Arthury, loopy way of sometimes sounding loopily right. I'm sitting with him one afternoon in the backyard of his new place. Two or three beers each. Some lazy, cagey chitchat . . . chummy, but always carefully easing away from the raw lip of the troublous spot. So long as we don't stray over that line, everything is up-tempo from him. I've seen his new bed and his new bold, floral shirt and his new bold, floral acrylic painting, and in sixty minutes I've heard his cell phone beep him into seven brief but mysterious smile-making conversations carried out in a hushed voice in the next room, and I've heard him tell me repeatedly how "every day is a new adventure," skimping on the sandwich fixings, figuring out the bank account: boom! awesome, enthralling, new adventures! I let my eyesight's edges loll about the house for signs of a woman . . . none. (Am I disappointed? Relieved?) But neither does he ask, not once from noon to five, how Martha's doing, nor wax nostalgic for a single halo'd molecule of the air they shared so long so well. I think the ring of vibrant yellow tufting dyed around his hair is a magic circle, intended to keep the past at bay—the past that needs to die in order for "new" to be born.

I'm thinking all that, and I'm lost in wishing I *did* possess a trove of psychobabble into which I could dip, when Martha (who never grows breathless on these walks, as I do) asks me, "What was that mythological animal?"

"Huh? Which one?"

"*That's* what I'm asking. The one that was made up from half parts of other animals."

"The basilisk."

"No . . . another one."

Centaur? Manticore? Pegasus? Griffin? Pan? . . .

"The griffin. I was thinking about how a marriage is really a creature fashioned patchily out of other lives. Like Frankenstein . . ."

"He's the doctor. You mean his monster."

". . . or the Minotaur or the griffin. Wasn't it something like a lion and a serpent?"—and before I can answer: "*Something like that. I was thinking how it all depends on whether the two parts stay together over time . . . who knows? A horse and bird wings—stupid*. But look at any illustration, and Pegasus is this gorgeous, airborne, exalted thing. Like a breath, with muscles. Then again, those freaking flying monkeys in *The Wizard of Oz* are sorry beasts. And Frankenstein turned out pretty altogether god-awful shitty."

"His monster."

I don't think it's my mild correction that suddenly has her weeping, stopping under one tree's overarching arms and weeping ashamedly into her own two hands; it isn't me who's caused this altogether god-awful shitty mess, and it isn't me who has the hoodoo to fix it. I'm only a friend who's standing next to a woman in peril. No last-minute balloon. And how can I look at that quicksand and hand her my small stone of foreboding?

If Catullus does offer a single incontrovertible view of marriage, it escapes my novice reading of that poet's oeuvre. If anything, the beast we call "monogamy" turns out to be—as the pages turn, and the cast of Catullus's characters go about their pleasures and miseries—as cobbled together as any griffin: sometimes contented and steadfast; often gusted by lust into treachery of one kind or another; and sometimes sing-the-blues conflicted over being so pied a beauty in a world of so many similar pinto-spotted, checkered, and mongrel attempts to be lifelong wedded for better or worse.

Poems 61, 62, and 64 are three of the lengthiest in the Catullus canon and three of the most ornate and delightful: even their jests are not so rough as those in his other poems, and their immediate occasions (again, as opposed to those of the other pieces) are grounded, the way that starlight is, in the constellated figures of gods and the implications of timelessness. All three concern marriages. Sixty-one serves well as their representative: here, in a choral piece of 225 lines (created in celebration of an actual wedding, Junia Aurunculeia to Manlius Torquatus), the speaker welcomes the overpresiding god of weddings, Hymen ("He brings us Venus the good; he is love's uniter"); lushly compliments the bride and groom on their beauty and on the fitness of their match; emboldens their spirits, should they be prone to the jitters; and reminds them that their days of lightweight love affairs are over, that a new, more important, and nourishing commitment is upon them now.

The erotic is admitted, yes, and its heats are even stoked ("Don't weep, Aurunculeia! Whoever wants to count the many thousand games of desire that will fall into your nights . . . let him first try to number Africa's sands!"). The poem is attitudinally *way* removed from being a paean to abstinence. But theirs will be a "virtuous passion," validated by family, by tradition, by the poet's own witnessing presence, and by the approval of

the participants' deities. There is no irony here. It's clear that Catullus intends his poem to honor the idea of formal nuptials: and he means us to see that sincerity, fidelity, and a durable mutuality flower out of this moment. These are, he tells us, "sacred rites."

Elsewhere (and more typically) in Catullus's poetry: fucking; sucking; and shucking off old lovers for new with a conscienceless ease. Sexual shenanigans—complete with deceit and depravity—abound; indeed, are the steaming entrée. This is the start (the First Triumvirate) of the darkly scandalous decades. A "well-known noblewoman invited three hundred orgiasts to a banquet" and was carried into the dining hall, nude, on a queenly platter, graped at her breasts and figged at her crotch and intended to be the main feast. A Calpurnius Bestia stood accused "of killing his wives—how many, not stated—by smearing a fast-acting poison on their vaginas as they slept." This is the field in which Catullus's poetic invention grazes and romps.

The beloved referred to, or addressed, in most of the poems is Clodia Pulcher, code-named Lesbia, an aristocrat and "enthusiast of sexual license." In this, she arrives with a pedigree: her father, Publius Clodius Pulcher, "is most often remembered as the young man who sneaked into an all-female religious festival, disguised as a flute girl, for an illicit meeting with Julius Caesar's wife." It was rumored that Lesbia and her brother were incestuous lovers. Another rumor: her husband, Metellus Celer, died by poison at her hand. Since she was adulterous as a wife (and Catullus would have been only one name in her schedule book of dalliances), it's no surprise that she became, as Mulroy phrases it, "a merry widow with an insatiable appetite for young men." In 58, one of his spiels of spite, the poet reports that Lesbia, "loved by Catullus more than he loved himself or all of his kin," is spending her time in the nooks of alleys skinning back the foreskins (and he doesn't mean for medical exams) of

a series of sleazily-come-by partners. Nor was *he* Mr. Faithful: "His poems imply unseemly extra-Lesbia entanglements with girls named Ipsithilla, Ameana, and Aufilena. In addition to this, he was infatuated with a boy named Juventius."

And so we have, at once, a body of poems in which the speaker can—with an articulate, genuine ardor—morosely observe how the gods have abandoned humankind ("Our mad confusion of everything fair with everything foul / has driven away their righteous and forgiving thoughts. They do not deign to visit any longer") *and* can glory at a face slobbered into some bodily crack like a truffle pig at work. Today, with Martha on my mind, this is a literary version of the griffin's composite anatomy, and it raises similar questions about how fated any alliance is; how pasted together with tissue paper and spit; how able to wake the next morning with ashes in its mouth and in the corners of its eyes and, like the phoenix, rise up anyway; how granite; how elastic; how bohemian; how cleaving to a norm. When do its differences know to yield to a greater good—and when do they squabble, slammingly pack their bags, and drive away to widely separated zip codes?

The hoofprint of a deer in snow: a perfect kiss.

The trail of such prints: a trail of perfect kisses, left by what we think of as a perfect creature, sleek and fleet, enabled in its leaps by some angelic oil suffusing its bones, a creature of one smooth piece, and of a piece with its surroundings.

But the griffin?—leaves the talon marks of an eagle; bears the hooked beak of an eagle, for a proud and ferocious prow of a face (*griffin* comes from *gryps*, Greek, "hooked"); has massively large, strong-tendoned wings; is partially feathered, black and cobalt and crimson—warrior colors; and has the torso of a lion, tipped by a lion's ears, a hint of mane, and a whipping tail . . . altogether an overpowering hodgepodge of an animal, albeit one known for a predator's strength and speed (in both running and flying): the tiger, the elephant, and the dragon will all succumb to the pounce of the griffin and its rending paws. It lays eggs. It constructs nests laced with threads of gold, "and these it protects" (the gold? or the eggs?) most vigorously. It confounds and beguiles and terrorizes: it haunts the night beyond the shepherds' comforting circle of campfire light.

Some mystifying ancestral line of the griffin's must have been in our heads, in the back cave-dark of our own heads, from at least Neanderthal times. The recognizably classic griffin makes its first appearance in Central Asian visual art around 3000 BC and its first appearance in written texts around 700 BC. Its amalgam body lends itself to a range of striking depiction—on brooches, on serving platters, about the bellies of bowls, on funerary caskets, as tattoos (a sign, for the Scythians, of lofty birth). And it's particularly a staple of medieval bestiaries, there with the fox and the boar and the weasel and the unicorn, and other real animals as described by the experts. Tenaciously, it remains in these books of lore past Shakespeare's day. (Dickens mentions a cynic who "in his hatred of men [is] a very griffin.") Catullus presumably could have expected to see an example in one of

Rome's newly founded *vivaria,* tethered for safety near the pit with the ragged tiger or by the column where the elephant was chained. The imperial gardens surely possessed one!

Classicist Adrienne Mayor posits that belief in the griffin was fueled by protoceratops remains, which "are so thick in that region, some researchers in the field regard them a nuisance. The prominent beak, large eyes and impressive claws . . . the body about the size of a lion's, the claws and long tail, the birdlike collarbone frill"—these are consistent with the anatomy claimed for the griffin. Plus, protoceratops laid eggs. "In many ways, the ancient people who came upon the bone fields of Central Asia were doing the same thing modern paleontologists do today—postulating unknown animals from ancient remains." Is it any less realistic than the platypus? (Than the couple next door, that devout fundamentalist kneeler-in-the-street and her atheist husband? Out of a skull filled with its superstition-powered hosts of devils and fluttering seraphs, and a skull filled with its one brisk whiff of a clear and rational ozone . . . comes this strange but functioning double-headed invention called "the neighbors." Try describing *that* in a bestiary across the page from the "cameleopard" or "cockatrice," and see if it isn't as credible.)

And in fact the griffin and all of its kin—all of the hybridized opposites, from real-life hermaphrodites to the fabled goat-footed people of northern Scythia and the dog-headed tribes of western Libya—hold a psychological value. They ease us through the horrors and astonishments of realizing that all of us lead dichotomized lives, and all of us (from the oxygenating red cells in our pulmonary systems to those pumping, gushing organs of our greatest physical ecstasies) are the stuff of amazing weddings, some metaphorical, some literal.

"Hold a psychological value"—yes. In her smart and snappy essay "The Terrible Griffin," Mahalia Way reminds her reader

"how important the preservation of conceptual dichotomies can be to a culture, how seminal they are to the way we understand the world to be ordered." Hesiod's account of the creation of the universe begins with Chaos, a word that first meant "undivided." And then of course, as in the Judeo-Christian tradition (and really *every* world mythology), division is made—light from dark, Earth from sky, land from sea—and by this act the universe is scaled to human comprehension, after which the divisions continue, people from animals, man from woman, etc. Maybe all of this only echoes the ur-division of Big Bang energy from out of the primordial singularity-dot . . . and afterward the original self-combining of that energy into elements.

Or in other words, one's culture is the child of a cosmos that itself was born of endless demarcation . . . so a culture will maintain the demarcation lines that clarify its values with the thorough-most of fervors. It will generate tales about the dangerous consequences of threatening essential distinctions (Eve and Adam, for instance, nearly "becoming like gods" by eating of the forbidden apple; ditto the overprideful labors behind the Tower of Babel). The culture will nurture myths about the taboo status of almost all transboundary beings (children produced by incestuous sex; the offspring of human–animal matings; all of the werewolves and vampires slinking about nefariously in the nethertwists of our brains; think octoroon in nineteenth-century New Orleans, think *The Island of Doctor Moreau* and its menagerie . . . no, "man-agerie"). And the culture will fabricate legends that also show weird admiration for, or even honor, some transboundary beings (here the androgyne is a fine example, lauded in alchemical texts as an emblem of twofold knowledge: or as in the song by Joni Mitchell, "I've looked at life from both sides now / From up and down . . .").

In many cultures, there's one day a year when the rigor with which we emphasize the lines is officially loosened, and men

will dress as women, women will parade about in the trousers of men, the madhouse gets unlocked, a fool in a dunce's cap is ushered into the mayor's sumptuous chair: these needs, these rich confusions, must be admitted. The rest of the year the sanctity of the lines is defended with every informal, religious, and legal muscle a culture can flex.

It wasn't uncommon in English villages of medieval times for premarital sex to be winked at by the authorities and, if anything, only lightly admonished. (The "legerwite," or lecherwite, a fine for premarital sex, was once as low as three pence in the Huntingdon village of Elton circa 1300; it never rose above twelve pence throughout that era. And a jury in Elton was fined by the local lord in 1316, charged with having failed to levy a fine at all in five proved cases of premarital hotcha hotcha.) Among the reasons: often enough, those indiscretions were simply a prelude to marriage and (given fertility) to family . . . they resulted in a proper boundaried unit of the community. *Adultery,* on the other hand, was severely punished: for peasants, a whipping. Obviously, adultery unpegs the squared-off corners of that same familial unit, and leaves it flapping away like a crazed wing on the squally winds of disorder, among the eddying ghosts, the demons and imps, that populate the air of this time and place and that tempt the frail will of people.

Mahalia Way: "Things that defy categorization exist. How is a culture to deal with them safely? Fascination with creatures who straddle dichotomies is itself a way of exploring and 'feeling' these divisions. The griffin served this purpose. As a hybrid of bird and beast, it represented both heaven and Earth, good and evil, God and Satan. It could be a mindlessly vicious aggressor—or plundered victim; a rapacious, vigilant hoarder—or a selfless, generous protector; a symbol of scientific knowledge—or of the sacred. In fact, the griffin has a lot to teach us about the process of interpretation."

For example: even my slow, lay reader's journey through Catullus gets stuck at forks in the interpretative road. Where Guy Lee uses "nipples" in Catullus 55 (the civil version, the "Doctor Jekyll" version), Mulroy opts for "tits" (the "Mister Hyde" choice). These are tonal worlds apart, and surely *one* of these is closer to the Roman poet's intention, but . . . I can only fuddle and muddle and shrug. I've already mentioned the venomous poem wherein a whorishly active Lesbia is "skinning" (i.e., rolling back the foreskins of) her alley clientele . . . or at least she is in Lee and Mulroy; Edith Hamilton, with only slightly more politeness, interprets "skinning" fiscally: Lesbia "on highways and byways seeks her lover, strips all Rome's sons of money."

If my friend Martha is going crazy, generating variorum interpretations of Arthur-stuff and rumored Arthur-stuff and dreamed-up Arthur-stuff . . . if Martha is sinking faster and with a more immediate woe on her lips than most of us . . . still, everyone I know has days (let's label them "interpretation days") when what they thought was solid ground below turns quicksand. As for all of those impressively credentialed claims for the widespread interbreeding of Neanderthals and *Homo sapiens:* "This interpretation has not gone unchallenged." Duarte (of the Portuguese Institute of Archaeology, in Lisbon) and Trinkaus (Washington University) say the child bones called Lagar Velho 1 "resulted from interbreeding." I've already told you that. *However . . .* Tattersall (the American Museum of Natural History, in New York) and Schwartz (of the University of Pittsburgh) "argue that Lagar Velho 1 is most likely 'a chunky *Homo sapiens* child,'" and only that.

More: in 1964, when Arno Penzias and Robert Wilson (radio engineers out testing a new, experimental antenna for satellite communications) stumbled upon the mysterious hiss we know now is the background radiation from the Big Bang, they were forced to eliminate all of the more expectably mundane causes,

including "a white dielectric substance" they'd found sticking to the equipment. Meaning: "pigeon shit." We fall from tonal world to tonal world; we sink, then bobble to the top, then sink again.

And here it comes, our symbol for *all* of this, making its way through an anecdote from the life of that genius of hokum and flimflam, P. T. Barnum. He'd purchased the Feejee Mermaid, but "the public must be made receptive first. It required a build-up." So Barnum hired his old friend Levi Lyman to stir the public press a bit, in Montgomery, Alabama, and Charleston, South Carolina, and Washington, D.C. This finally resulted in Lyman's bringing the Feejee Mermaid to New York and Philadelphia while disguised as a dignified British representative of the Lyceum of Natural History in London. The editors ate it up! Their readers were thrilled and expectant! And the name that Barnum and Lyman had concocted for their bogus British duster-offer of stuffed exotic hummingbirds and arranger-by-size of old bones? . . . Dr. *Griffin*.

This summer Yancy is one bright chip in a kaleidoscope: along with other scintillant chips called Amy and Della and Elinore and Leslie and Raven and Nora (and more), he's part of an ever-morphing confettiesque flower bed of *amor*. (Hey, he's *my friend*. He's not "a predator upon women's affections," not "an opportunist." He's a salt lick in the wilds, and the deer draw near in a mesmerized queue. He's a dollop of pollen: the bees go nuts. He's a saint in blotchy silhouette in the center of a tortilla, and the faithful flock from miles away to bake themselves in the rays of the One and Only True Tortilla.) There's a lot of midnight jasmine tea and bedspring-jounce at Yancy's house.

At Ed's house there's a lot of Ed. One night, when the echoes of loneliness are especially unbearable, Ed invites me over to share a recently purchased twelve-pack of beer and a two-gallon drum of Chocolate-Rum-Pistachio Fantasia ice cream, also a retro-trip through the groovy 45s of his adolescence ("My God!—the Association!!! *Cherish!*"). It's fun. Or at least, it's the fun edge of desperation: *my* companionship isn't what Ed needs. What's the matter here? He's likable. He's as tender as underdone veal. Aren't women *always saying* that's what they're searching for? "Right. As they kick off their slingbacks and head out the door with Mr. Arrest Record." Ed drops into a fitful snooze around 3:00 a.m., and I let myself out. In the quiet of his driveway, I imagine I can hear (about . . . let's see now . . . seven miles away) a gentle duo of satiated snores from Yancy's bedroom.

Yes, but *all* of that is only a muffled murmur in the background of (as it's known in the office) the Soon-to-Be-Fateful Summer of Sweet and Danny. They're suddenly *everywhere*. Not as a couple, exactly: it's frustrating. An example—I'm chatting with Arthur in the parking lot of our neighborhood Stop-N-Go store: motor-rev, kid yowling, gas fumes, angry curses, a rising escalator of ladylaughter, breaking glass . . . the usual, and *boing!* here's Sweet with her weightless field of corn-silk hair in

the breeze that attends her, waving nonchalantly to me as she walks out with a twenty-ounce Summer Sipper cup of cherry punch. *Hey Sweet, hi, do you know Arthur, how's it going, take care,* and she slips her lusciously bare legs into the front seat of her low-slung and electrically scarlet speedster with the single thoughtless flip of a dolphin diving. As she turns the engine . . . Danny ("Just coincidence?" Sandi the secretary asks of me the following day, "or [here, a pencil drumroll on the desk] the Wheels of Destiny?") pulls into the lot three spaces away and waves to us all with a smile, and—as Sweet screeches out into noontime traffic—enters the store for his own cool drink. For me the whole thing squeaks like a narrative straining to break from its pupal case.

Let's roll, guys. Office memo to Sweet and Danny: *Tempus fugit, carpe diem.* One day last week they arrived at the office wearing the same style of knit shirt (hers, a lavender; his, a navy blue) and—the dopes—*they seemed oblivious to this portentous fact.* The rest of us weren't: all that day the pencil drumroll followed the travel of each of them through our office mazelet of desks. We've done our research, people: neither of you is "seeing anybody else." Let's step on the gas! Let's pop the first of the many potential sequential sexual questions! Let's rumble! They go about their workday in their independent sugar-spun fogs . . . Let's rock! Let's make evolution happen!

Some afternoons I'm tempted to waylay Danny in the supplies room and unfold for him a lovingly detailed road map toward the Country of Sweet. *Albert "Cupid" Goldbarth. No Poor Schmo Too Hopeless, No Lothario Too Chock-Full of Success! A Free Service.* I'm tempted, but I don't. I'm tempted not only because these two were imprinted, each with the other's image, somewhere around the zygote stage, but also because I think (and it's unanimous) that Danny's . . . well, "a good guy," in the forthright words of Sandi, our office's Peerer into the Souls of

Men. He's hunky, and yet he hasn't been tainted by locker-room garbage-talk. He's still a somewhat unformed lump of manhood, but the raw material's rich with the glints of an honest smile and steadfast gaze.

I think of him in the way Edith Hamilton thinks of the young Catullus. For almost every other commentator, the poems and the poet behind them mean a carnal capability for the nitty-grittier, demimondish side of our behavior. And maybe, okay, he *did*, under Lesbia's wickedly appetitive tutelage, eventually embody that disposition. (She would have provided effective schooling.) But when he first arrived in Rome from Verona, "sent by a careful father to be cultivated and polished out of small town ways, [Catullus] was perhaps twenty or so. We must conceive him on his first entrance a very shy young provincial, hesitating on the edge of [big city] company." For Hamilton his first response to Lesbia's attention was "the holy purity of a great love. A passion conceived of as eternally faithful has always been felt to be its own justification, and through his life Catullus loved Lesbia only." Ah . . . ! What if his emotions had been stirred by someone worthier, by someone like . . .

Sweet ambles past with the boss's request for a jumbo box of paper clips in her hands. On empty afternoons I'm likewise tempted to waylay *her* and likewise drag her into the supplies room for a mini-lecture on love and Danny and ways goddammit to be a little more directed, please, in her thus-far aimless float-ing amidst the birds and the bees.

I'm tempted, sure; but again I don't. In the first place . . . spotless soul though I am, you'd be surprised at how many col-leagues of mine would cast a cynical eye upon that innocuous attempt to be alone with Sweet in the confines of the supply room. They're a drag-ass, mealy-spirited bunch, but still I under-stand: the air around her is as clear as fresh springwater . . .

and as potent as booze. And anyway, in the second place, thirty-five years separate us. I don't speak Sweetish.

If I could, I'd knock their silly heads together; the ensuant spark might profitably land in their tinder and lead to an appropriate conflagration. The weather is right for this; the wind is right; the conditions for this benevolent, righteous fire are at their likeliest. *Oh flame, oh flame, oh little itty-bitty knock* . . . It's tempting, but I don't. It rarely works in the buttinsky's favor—everybody knows this. In Aston, Bedfordshire, in the late 1200s, the village records show that "Robert Haring and his wife Sybil fell to quarreling." Then, says *Life in a Medieval Village,* "a friend eating lunch with them tried to intervene as peacemaker, and"—let this be a lesson for one and all—"was slain by an axe blow."

"Shotgun wedding": we all know the term. In the village of Elton in 1300 it would have been, I guess, a "pitchfork wedding." The sadness is always the same: the narrowing of the options in a life. Not that I advocate one's ditching the responsibility often born of a cautionless whoopee. Even so, it's possible to recommend that one take up the burdens of his or her unasked-for and sudden, sullen adulthood—recommend it with a sanctimonious heartihood—and still understand how suffocating the grip of that circumstance feels. Springsteen has it just right in his song "The River": "Then I got Mary pregnant / And man, that was all she wrote. / And for my nineteenth birthday / I got a union card and a wedding coat." His raspy, almost choking voice and the music to match: yet another man and woman have entered the roll call of the living dead. The dulling factory job. The tonnage of laundry. A horribly long-term payment for a single hour of pleasure.

But the genes don't care if we're miserable: the genes want more and better genes, and therefore want as many possible combinations of genes as they can force from us. They want that child. They want a cultural institution inside of which that child will grow to fulfill its own fate in the procreative nature of things. We live inside these culturally inherited lines—at least most of us do—and we stare down their iron, unwavering train-track length to what we call the horizon, and see . . . well, you know what we see: at their end the tracks are so close together, they're going to squeeze us dry. And so we also understand (even if we don't recommend it) the gesture of fugitive celebration when one of Springsteen's other speakers leaps out of the lines, in "Hungry Heart": "Got a wife and kids in Baltimore, Jack. / I went out for a ride and I never went back."

Springsteen's speakers—the out-of-work and the out-of-wedlock, the flunkies and junkies, the part-time roofers, late-night-diner waitresses, racetrack hustlers, red-eye fliers, experts

in petty theft and broken dreams and stolen kisses—know (whether intellectually or out of hard-knocks experience) the power of cultural hierarchy. Lines: in "Atlantic City," the speaker—whose choices in life are all used up, who's betting his future against one last suspicious (and, as the listener comes to understand, doomed) favor for a friend—is a streetwise scholar of the importance of heeding categories: "Down here it's just winners and losers and don't get caught on the wrong side of that line."

When the lines between permitted and unpermitted foods were established in Deuteronomy and Leviticus, they were established (so far) forever: thousands of years in the future, my father would be helplessly gagging up his food in public and spitting it out, on discovering—some swallows too late—that pork was part of the recipe. (An old-time Woolworth's soda fountain counter remains my most embarrassing memory of such moments.) The aversions attaching to kosher run deep. My own first encounter with shrimp, at thirteen, left me retching in a men's room: *shrimp!*—those delectably meaty paisleys of the sea I've eaten since then *thousands* of times, in dozens, hundreds, of creative preparations, and always with gusto.

In *Purity and Danger,* Mary Douglas deconstructs the rationale behind the dietary rules—the rules of defilement and accordance in matters of food choice—as instructionally dictated in the Old Testament. "You shall not eat any abominable things . . . ," the camel, the hare, the rock badger, the swine, the buzzard, the carrion vulture, the stork, the mouse, the gecko, the weasel, the cormorant, and a "zoo who's who" of other prohibited creatures of every footed, finned, and bewinged stripe. Then a similar, smaller list of the properly edible: the ox, the sheep, the goat, the wild ibex, certain locusts (and yet not *any* locusts), the frog, the roebuck, and others. What's the actual methodology here, so powerful that millennia later it toggled

my father's gag reflex? In an earlier chapter Douglas has prepared us for the answer when she says, "Ideas about separating, purifying, and punishing transgressions have as their main function to impose system on an inherently untidy experience. It is only by exaggerating the difference between within and without, above and below, male and female, with and against, that a semblance of order is created."

Later she turns to Deuteronomy and Leviticus strictures. First, she argues, they aren't primarily early guidelines for a healthy diet (the "tapeworm thesis"). Nor are they primarily an attempt at defining the Jewish tribe by contrast to neighboring peoples (*"they* eat such-and-so, those filthy-dick pigfuckers, but *we* eat so-and-such"). Instead, she says, it's a straightforward matter of realizing that "holiness" is defined for biblical Judaism "as wholeness and completeness." Ideally every aspect of personal and social life would serve to reflect this principle of unity, and Douglas provides a number of examples.

Sacrificial animals must be "without a blemish." A priest of the tribe "may not come into contact with death"—his commitment to life must be one hundred percent. A warrior who experienced a nocturnal emission, a woman menstruating, are to be quarantined away from the population: in *our* language their bodies have ceased to be "closed systems" so have temporarily given up their natural perfection. A man who has started to build a house but not completed it, or planted a vineyard and not yet tasted the fruit of its wine, or wedded but not yet consummated the marriage . . . these are unfit to go into battle: they must first fulfill the earlier totality. "You shall not let your cattle breed with a different kind; you shall not sow your field with two kinds of seed; nor shall there come upon you a garment of two bemixed sortings of cloth. Be holy [complete], for I am holy [complete]."

And the same for one's menu selection. "Holiness," says Douglas, "requires that individuals conform to the class to which

they belong . . . and requires that different classes of things shall not be confused." So four-footed creatures that fly are imperfect members of a grouping and thus unfit for consumption. An animal that has two hands and yet still locomotes on all fours like a quadruped is unclean. And "'swarming' is not a mode of propulsion proper to any [one particular] element; swarming things are neither fish, flesh nor fowl. Eels and worms inhabit water, though not as fish; reptiles go on dry land, though not as quadrupeds; some insects fly, though not as birds. There is no order in them." (In this formulation a badger isn't a mammal; it's a fraction, of two discordant halves. Or in Marthan-and-Arthurian terms, its parts aren't wedded persuasively and coherently.) One by one Douglas ticks down the list, and every animal's status is explained in the light of her theory. And the bottom line? "The dietary laws would have been like signs which at every turn inspired meditation on the oneness, purity and completion of God."

Is this a case of overkill in response to unbearable knowledge? Maybe a people's God is required to be so whole, and his people so unreservedly pledged to a mimetic wholeness, only because some last remaining lucid intuition-node in the back of the brain suspects that in reality the Creator of this universe is conflicted *in his own* wants and intentions. To suspect such a frightening thing is to need immediately to deny it, with every atom of our zealousness.

It is *this* God, the maker but also the breaker of covenants; the one who stands above all petty bickering but admits to being a jealous and vengeful Lord; the one who makes man in his image, and in so doing makes a creature bound to disappoint; the birther of us, and the smiter of us, the one who demands our trust and yet, untrusting, repeatedly tests us; the sexual prude for whom our profligate reproduction is a sign of his favor; the one who giveth and taketh away, who asks of us

both love and fear, who demands to be known by us in all of his terror and glory and also to be *un*knowable . . . *this* is Jack Miles's God, in his book *God,* and it makes for a compelling (and somewhat scary) read. Essentially conflict occurs in our lives because of "the conflict of good and evil" in the character of God himself.

If this is true, is it any wonder we stumble through Springsteenian workplace days and desperate (or boozy, bluesy, spunk-and-fury-fueled) Springsteenian nights with feelings about the lines of our lives that—in the calmest of us, even—often appear as diagnosably bipolar? We yo-yo crazily from middle-class conformity to jailbreak rebellion and then back. We envy the family man. We envy the footloose wanderer. We keep our good-guy noses to the grindstone, and we keep our wise-guy eyes out for a piece of ass. We sing our hallelujahs in a great praise for "the ties that bind"; we sing in great self-pity of "the chains of love"—they are, of course, the same one thing but modulated according to whatever the zing of the moment is. We lullaby and ai-yi-yi and oy and okeydokey.

Is it any wonder we turn to each other and ask that our bodies supply and receive some solace? (Or is that only what the genes would have us think, for their own reasons?) Just as someone, somewhere, knows how mortal flesh yearns to be mingled with spirit . . . so do Springsteen's speakers know the urge of the flesh to be jazzed up with a counterbalancing flesh, shuffled together, lost and found and combo'd out of themselves for a night or a lifetime and into a new thing.

On a bottle's label: Shake Well Before Using.

The hill land pasture is higher than he's taken his sheep in a while. No practical reason brought him here this morning, just the increasingly wonderful lavender hues of the hill land itself, which deepened as he rose along the rocky trail, leading him on as if *he* were a sheep, leading him by the eyes, by beauty. "Shit Nose," and he snaps his fingers. Shit Nose is an affectionate name that he's given his dog—his herder dog, his more-to-him-than-his-own-right-arm. The dog abandons its one especially funkily gunked-up tuft of hill land weeds and gives him a look, the equivalent of "Huh?" "Shit Nose," and he moves his hand in a circle that means to admire the whole increasingly lavender vista, "this is . . . ," then he falls silent. Swept entirely into a momentary sublimity he may be, but his vocabulary—he's an ancient Scythian—is weak on words accommodating grandeur in Nature's showcase.

Indeed, for an ancient Scythian, Nodor is rather dreamy. The typical Scythian is a badass slice-your-nuts-off guy, an up-yours-momma guy. The men are known not only as archers of fearlessness and accuracy; they attach thorns to their arrowheads and coat them in a potent mixture of rotting adders, dung, and putrefied blood. They tan the hides of vanquished enemies, then use them for clothing, towel rags, shield coverings; the cranium of an enemy makes a drinking vessel of stylish appeal. A woman must kill an enemy in battle as a prerequisite to marriage. I said the *typical* Scythians. Up in the hills are flocks (or is it prides?) of griffins, eager for meat (*these* hills, our Nodor realizes queasily, ending his reverie), and according to rumor, Scythian bandits, outlawed from the tribal units, still use these hills as a headquarters: what do *they* care for carnivore griffins!

So it's no surprise that Nodor's life is his shepherding. (*Some* person in this rough, nomadic culture has to do it—but no one of stature.) There are streaks of Scythian fierceness in him, certainly: both nature and nurture have seen to that. But these are

counterweighted, or more, by a tendency toward gentleness and a penchant for daydream. It wasn't an easy childhood; it's astounding that he *survived* childhood. In any case, his marriage didn't survive long past the oaths sworn over the ritual, shared drinking-skull. (In this formulation, a marriage isn't a unit of two people, but a fraction of two discordant halves.) Sometimes he feels as if there are two, or three, or ten (and here his counting ability ceases) Nodors, sewn together with only the coarsest of skill. And so we meet him up here, in the thinner hill land air, alone and thoughtful.

But it isn't only the height and the stone and the meadow flowers that give this lonely place its lavender coloration. It's also the hill land light, which, quicker than Nodor's eye has realized, deepens into a dusky plum, and then a gray, and then an impenetrable obsidian. He won't be returning his sheep to the fold, it looks like, so he gets them loosely penned inside a natural circle of rocks he finds conveniently at hand, then lights a fire for himself, to push the chilly touch of that besieging obsidian a little farther away. "Here, Shit Nose." Out of the pouch, a dried rind for himself and one for his weed-exploring companion. And then: strange noises, faintly, from out of the surrounding mystery zone. Like claws on tile. Like grunts from an inhuman throat. A whine from Shit Nose now: alert and not entirely courageous.

It's a thickly Persian-lamb night sky. The darkness all around him is a thin black shell, and, yes, he's sure, there are sounds of . . . something. Something on the other side of that black shell, trying to break through. Nodor has a stick, his only weapon. He lifts it now, although without much confidence. He's never seen one of these dangerous beasts but grew up with their stories and their images, and he isn't too heartened. Even so, with a dry-mouthed swallow he wills the battle-lust part of himself, the thirster for blood from a living body, up from its psychic hiding place.

More claw-click . . . thudding . . . a grunt rising into a howl . . . And the black shell shatters, and horror itself steps through. There are three of them. Everything is fast, and flickered by firelight, and made a blur by fright, but he sees the savage beaks and the wings and the scourging tails . . . one of them clubbing Shit Nose into unconsciousness, another beginning to club the sheep, to splatter them into death . . .

A club? And Nodor sees, in his panicked, shadowed, adrenaline-crazy version of seeing: the beaks descend from masks, the wings are strapped on, and the tails are parts of shabby, belted-on animal pelts. "Griffins are people," he thinks. He whirls, he ducks, he deftly jumps out into the darkness— now for a minute *his,* not *their,* enabler—and he runs, and then runs more, and he doesn't stop until his lungs seem emptied of the ability to inhale, and it's really only coincidence that by the time he falls in a heap to the dark dirt in the dark air of this dark night of his life, the frightening sounds of pursuit are long gone. He gives a few weak pukes, then lies there sobbing, doing a dead man's float on the ground. When the sobbing has wrung him dry, he blanks out. When he comes to, it's still up-the-asshole dark, but there's the slobbery nudge of Shit Nose all over his face, and some revivifying licking.

Shit Nose—is alive! And he, *he,* Nodor, is alive! And he really did handle himself with a fierce adroitness! Nodor the shepherd handled himself with a warrior adroitness! And before he blanks out for a final time, Shit Nose standing guard, he remembers saying "—or people are griffins."

There's a version of the legend of Theseus similar in its intent: another story of confrontation with a monster that leads to a moment of self-understanding. But in Theseus's case, the hero proves a disappointment.

Catullus zeroes in on Theseus's fall from our admiration in

the longest of his pieces to have survived, the marriage poem we number 64 and which the poet himself may well have considered his masterpiece. An epyllion—in effect a miniature epic—of 408 lines, the poem imagines the wedding of Peleus and Thetis ("When the long-awaited light of this chosen day appears, the entire region of Thessaly throngs to the palace!"). If marital unions bridge the separation between two lives, and then combine their differences, *this* love-pairing out of Greek mythology is a paragon of the distance such a bridge can span: Thetis, a goddess (sea nymph daughter of Nereus, an ocean god), is going to swear her troth in marriage to Peleus, a mortal man. It's a doozy of a synchrony and a glorious occasion.

The poem, however, uses the marriage as a framing device, devoting more space to other, interior narratives. For example, a vibrant tapestry arrayed upon "the nuptial bed of the goddess" is "embroidered with old-time human figures" enacting some of the history of Theseus and Ariadne. Whatever his reasons, Catullus chooses *not* to retell the moment of high adventure when Theseus triumphs over the savage man-bull Minotaur in its labyrinth down in the bowel of the world, and he *doesn't* (as would be appropriate for the blanket over a wedding night's explorings) let us linger on the early love of Ariadne and Theseus: after all, without that love, and what it means of her decisive aid, there is no triumph down in the dung-filled, spiraling Minotaur warrens.

Instead, Catullus has this coverlet show the scene, much later on, where Theseus abandons Ariadne on an island—she's of no use to him now—and sails alone into what he believes will be a golden future. Ariadne, "emerging from treacherous sleep," finds herself "on an empty beach, deserted," and "she sees what she sees, but she hardly believes that she sees it." Her hurt is immense ("her entire heart and soul and dissolving mind hung

upon you, Theseus"), and soon so is her anger ("a fire engulfed her entire frame, igniting the depths of her being, her innermost marrow"). What follows is her long-term, virulent cursing not only of that king-of-all-ingrates Theseus but also of anyone forthcoming in his genealogical line: *nobody* does scorn and high dudgeon better than Catullus's Ariadne. "As my grievance is real and my tears are wrung from my heart, oh gods and goddesses, do not allow my sorrow to languish forgotten, but let the heedless mind of Theseus cause death and destruction to him and his kin!"

All this because—as she says in addressing the dot of his ship as it slips swiftly toward the horizon—"you raised up lying expectations in my piteous heart of married happiness, longed-for hymeneals . . . all of which, the winds have tattered now into nothingness." With all of Greek mythology at his disposal, this is a strange choice of Catullus's for a poem in celebration of a wedding. Unless he means it to serve as a kind of poetry lightning rod, a story to attract the gods' laments and censures, thus keeping the house of Peleus and Thetis safe from these. Or it's the necessary contrast, we could say, by which the unending delight of Peleus and Thetis will forever be able to measure itself. (The dirty question: is this the way Martha and Arthur work for the rest of us?) This makes some sense since, as we know, we're reading a poet who himself has been perpetrator and victim, lambkin, stalking wolf, destroyer and destroyed, on love's unstoppably revolving wheel of roles.

And so in the version of the adventure that I was referring to, Theseus—still of virtuous motivation and brave heart at this moment—stands victorious, panting, wounded, over the fresh corpse of that hideous conglomeration, the Minotaur, and witnesses in its dimming eyes . . . his own face mirrored back at him, with a sense *of its being at home there.* A premonition, perhaps. A glimmer of self-analysis, perhaps, and an admission of

confusion. As if any action the beast could imagine, Theseus could imagine too.

One day Danny stays home with a cold. How can his undeclared devotion stand it, being away from her presence? How can *she* stand it? Everyone's invisible-but-capable curiosity antennae are erect and on their highest sensitivity settings. Will Sweet reveal, whether overtly or through scattered dozens of smaller clues, that she misses him? *That's* stupid; *of course* she misses him! All year they've been doing their pas de deux in pirouetted arabesques that sometimes swing them to opposite sides of the office, or even (when out on various errands) opposite sides of town, but always attached by gossamer strands that stretch to the point where they can't be seen, yet exhibit a tensile strength that won't allow the pairing to break apart. *We know it!* But will she admit it today, in little acts of this or that? Sandi: *yes.* Sean: *no.* Juanita: *yes.* Sweet is oblivious to this, as she makes her cream-and-honey way around the office, but she's a Rorschach test for the rest of us.

Heading back from lunch, I find her lazing on the front steps, sipping dreamily out of a Styrofoam cup, on coffee break alone and seemingly pondering something mesmerizing exposed in the tarry bottom of the cup. The sun is pleased to gleam on her bare legs; I can almost hear it congratulating itself on this good fortune.

"Hey, Sweet."

"Hey, Albert." So I sit down too, figuring that "Hey, Albert" counts as a heartfelt invitation. Some people do *like* talking to me—unburdening themselves. I may be of help here. I may even leave with something choice for Sandi or Ron or Shonika to chew on.

"What's up, Sweet?"

She doesn't answer right away. People pass by; a few clouds

tease the sun and then give up on that game; a sparrow considers a cigarette butt, its head cocked to one side with the serious tilt of an airport security guard who's just discovered an abandoned suitcase. She's thinking: how trustworthy am I, will I laugh at her? (no), will I tell the others? (well, maybe). She cocks her head too.

"I think I'm in love. Is that crazy or what?"

"Not crazy. Why shouldn't you be in love?"

"Or not in love, exactly. But I have to tell you: I have this big crush on someone. That's it: I'm in crush."

"Do I know him?"

"*Do* you! Remember that day at the Stop-N-Go? He's that friend of yours, what's-his-name. Flowery shirt. Art, right? With the thingy of blond-tint spikes."

Arthur.

We are so royally screwed-up, we human beings.

One week the rains come in; they *own* this city. They hose this city clean of everything else and fill it with only themselves. Every hour is rain o'clock. Gray ghosts of the rain leak through our basement walls. And then, in a day, it's gone. The sun takes over: the new regime, as bad as the last one. Everything bakes. A car is like a brick just out of the oven. Getting into a car is like entering the center of oven heat. Rain, sun, rain, sun, a story of how the president lied to us, a story of third-world people looking to better their lives by slitting our throats, day, night, drought, flood, a heartwarming story of child-A who was cured of fatality-Z, dark, light, stability, flux, the summer of com-, recom-, and uncombining.

It's also the summer of *The Incredible Hulk,* that blockbuster special effects box office hoo-ha-ha of a hit. You know, the movie of the original Marvel comic book of the same name: milquetoast Dr. Bruce Banner is . . . something, what is it? Irradiated or something, caught in a comet's tail or something, and now whenever he grows angry—*wham!* He jolts, beyond controlling, into a green humongous rampaging thing, all vein-snaked sacks of muscle and teeth that want to chew rocks for practice before they get to the bad guys' throats.

Which is really a way of saying it's the summer of Robert Louis Stevenson's Jekyll and Hyde, redone in cartoon garishness. Stevenson predates Freud with his insight (that the bull-man of the labyrinth still roams the brains of all of us and waits to be let out, a violent, infantile, irrational genie: "Don't rub me," the saying goes, "the wrong way"), but the marriage of human and animal predates Stevenson by millions of years, and is there in the umbers and smoky blacks of the earliest representational art we know, in the caves, where stag and shaman, cow and fertility goddess, ox and Paleolithic hunter, are made as one and perform their untranslatable rites.

"The marriage of human and animal"—*marriage.* You see?

It's the summer of Martha and Arthur, who provide the major structuring image through which my hazy conjectures approach all things. Like reading a recent essay on Jung: "The integration of conscious and unconscious contents creates a balanced perspective known as the 'self.'" Is the "self" a marriage, then, of two distinct but binary-system partners? If so would a "centered self" (in the language of buzzword therapy) be the same as a "happy marriage" (in the language of Joe and Jill from down the block)? Is this metaphor helpful at all? The summer of the Hulk, of Ed, of Yancy, the unending summer of Martha and Arthur.

What's also a brilliant understanding from popular horror storytelling is when, in the original Frankenstein movie by director James Whale, the standard destructiveness–tenderness polarity is reversed, and instead of being reminded yet again that a monster resides in the souls of even the kindliest among us, we see the equally true opposite: the monster, newly risen from the laboratory table of his creation, raises his hands in an innocent wonder at the sunlight, trying to hold it, softly mewling. For all of his bolts and sunken glower, for all of the plain fact that his body is really a *scrimmage* of other bodies, he's as freshly formed as a butterfly drying its wings of the damp of its birth throes. Later, we'll see his attempts to play with a little girl in the village, one of the movie's few other scenes where sunlight is allowed to touch the monster (there's no agenda involved, except his desire for happy community). Is he "sensitive"?—in the second of Whale's Frankenstein movies, the monster sits, with a rapt and obvious fulfillment, through a violin rendition of "Ave Maria" (and in the novel, you'll remember, he has the desire and time to learn French).

And still he's doomed to become the murder-thirsty, lumbering thing implied by his grab-bag origins, his brain-from-here-and-liver-from-over-there parody of our own beginnings.

"Lumbering," "murder-thirsty" . . . and desperately lonely. Wise in the ways of the mind, the novel exhibits how much of the monster's savagery is really a reaction to the institution of marriage (or to community of any sort) and his exclusion from it. (*"Everybody's* got a hungry heart," says Springsteen. Even, evidently, if it's transplanted.) The promise of companionship arises when Victor Frankenstein begins work on a second of his odious fabrications—but "during a sudden attack of scruples, he destroys his handiwork, infuriating the monster" (Martin Tropp), who runs off (actually, sails away across the Irish Sea) with this threat: "I shall be with you on your wedding night." True enough, the wedding night eventually comes around, and the monster is there to strangle Frankenstein's childhood sweetheart, Elizabeth.

James Whale's movie version *also* tantalizes the monster with a vision of companionship. Most of us can readily picture Elsa Lanchester tilted up on her table ("She's alive! ALIVE!") and then unbandaged, giving us an eyeful of her electrodynamically frizzled wings of hair—the intended bride. And yet on seeing the intended groom, she recoils, as anybody would, and the monster can all too clearly read the leaping disgust in her eyes. In its way the scene is heartrending. *How could* he have imagined being wedded to her, when *his own self* isn't a seamlessly unified entity? (I think of a poem from a student, Lindsay McQuiddy: "My face is sliding off of me, / a leaf of skin . . ."). His own bones, heart, lungs, skull, and pods of nerves are uneasy cohabitants, and some days they must feel as irreconcilable as a Brahmin (who "will not eat ginger or onion: for these are grown in the ground") and one of the same religion's *achuta*, "untouchables," whose work is to unclog raw shit from the sewers in Indian villages—by hand—or cremate the dead or sweep up the dung from the streets (one subset group is called the Musahar, "the rat eaters": you can imagine). There was

a time within living memory when an untouchable would be beaten *if his shadow touched* a person from a higher caste. Now Frankenstein's monster looks in the mirror: his left eye and his right eye want to file for divorce.

Although ample evidence also exists that meldings of otherwise piecemeal portions *can* be truly incorporative and greater than the mere sum of their parts: can be a *marriage* in the sense that Martha means in her more dogged spates of optimistic thinking. Mahalia Way suggests one function of the griffin was to serve as—and *because of,* not despite, its multi-speciesness—a symbol of Totality: to that extent, it was paid reverence. The same is true of the pangolin—an "actual" animal filling the role of the mythological griffin. Mary Douglas: "The pangolin or scaly ant-eater contradicts all the most obvious animal categories. It is scaly like a fish, but it climbs trees. It is more like an egg-laying lizard than a mammal, yet it suckles its young. And most significant of all, unlike other small mammals, its young are born singly, in the nature of humans. In its own existence it combines all the elements which the Lele culture normally keeps apart, and so suggests a meditation on the inadequacy of the categories of human thought. It achieves a union of opposites. It overcomes the distinctions in the universe." She calls it a "benign monster."

Could *any* of this be of use to my friends? To Cissy and Will, who are just back from their road trip to the Smoky Mountains, "now that the kids are grown and out of the house"—and so are the flocks of spooks, suspicions, and selfishly yammering demands that filled their heads for the first two decades of their life together? To Cynthia, at the singles mixer "opera night"? (Not that "karaoke night" and "casino night" were successes.) To Ben, who's waiting for Reese to show up with his bail? Out of all of this, is there a gift I can bring to them, a clarity? The summer days accumulate; the summer nights are a sour, black

murk on top. The summer of Martha and Arthur, still no closer to reconciliation *or* to a terminal split. The days are long; if light can have an echo, then these summer days are it, as they keep bouncing off the darkness with unwillingness to fade. Then finally the moon comes out, and it juggles even that leftover light. And the moon that we see in the river, which is a lie of a moon, also juggles *its* light accordingly: which is, I suppose, a version of truth. Tharur and Armtha, Athra and Marthur. The summer of griffins being reported everywhere, their bodies built completely of synesthesia, of all of your photographs of bygone lovers you tore one night and let the wind remix and marry. Who knows—what unfathomably expert chemist of human savors and human dreams will *ever* know—the extant combinations that can rain down from the potentialsphere, sinking into our little garden hearts and briefly flourishing there?

I only wanted to look at the simple question, "What is and isn't a proper coupling?" You read it so many pages ago. Now, after Greek gods, P. T. Barnum, ancient laws of *kosherkeit,* nostalgia rock . . . the various tributaries that feed this question, here we are, Tharma, Rathur, Mathrum, Amthur, trading our carbon dioxide for the oxygen of the Hill Park trees. It's the boggled-up summer of all this; and it all comes down, like a fine silt, to the delta of marital imagery. "I haven't called him in over a week" or "Why do I hear he's buying new shirts?" It's sunny out, and we go for our walk. It rains, we don our hooded, rubberized ponchos, and we go for our walk. We do what we can. We read great works. We ring our bells and buzzers.

The genes, the aether, the mystically charged gestalt, the elemental subparticles of the fire in the hearts of stars . . . we have to understand that we're arrangements of What's Out There, we're the way What's Out There comprehends itself and grows. We're temporary; we'll be rearranged—sometimes apparently for the better, sometimes not. But that we will be re-

arranged is certain. We will go to pieces and be repieced; this is inevitable. That we will rest, be stable for a while, in a shape that pleases . . . this can happen too, in its turn. Luck helps but isn't a guarantee. Intelligence helps but isn't a guarantee. Sometimes we're hammered into a thousand slivers, each with its pain. Sometimes we're still, and the world around us is still, and a small joy asks if we want to break out of this stillness and dance. Who knows why?—sometimes it all works out.

One evening I visit Mister J and George, out on their front porch. The moon is full. Tonight it can juggle a thousand plates of light, or more, and not drop one. Since Mister J is known for his micro- (read here: *one-small-screened-off-portion-of-musty-basement*) brewery, we're enjoying a third apiece of his latest triumph in the world of malts and hops. The two of them seem so pleased, and I let myself feel complicitous in their pleasure. The sounds surrounding us are mainly those of a difficult city—slams of cars and howls of sirens and far-off factory rumblings—but the thinnest hum of cricket-mantra from out in back is like the application of a lubricant that allows these giant gears to engage. We've been talking tonight about dozens of things and dozens of people we know in common. Suddenly I find myself asking them, "How do you do it, stay together?"

George leans close with his secret juju wisdom. "It's because I've volunteered to take out the garbage on Wednesdays."

"Oh right," Mr. J chimes in. "Like puffball here knows what it's like to hustle off of his little foofoo fairy-ass and *sacrifice*."

There's a second of silence. And then at once from both of them, with eventually my accompaniment, is the laughter of people lucky in love, that leaves us like an invisible keyboard trilling its music on up to the sky.

Later that summer I'm prepping for a fall undergraduate course that I teach on poetics.

Sometimes the skeleton and the skin of a poem are inseparable from its subject—that's the best, I tell them. Think of a poem that is spoken to us by somebody in a straitjacket, and it's tightly rhymed, A-A, B-B. Or a long poem overspilling its lines, spoken by a cokehead. I remind them of Catullus 56—the poem (as a student of rowdy intelligence once put it) where he stuffs it into Lesbia's slave's back hole—and then I read to them out of Ross King's book *Ex-Libris,* about "the lone parchment of the works of Catullus that had been found . . . bunging up a wine barrel in a tavern in Verona." Some metaphors won't let go. "There are many things I don't know," I say, "but trust me: I know how to recognize the marriage of form and content."

A Cave in a Cliff in Scotland

1.

"Troll/human or elf/human marriages almost never work, and their children are always torn between two worlds," says Fonn in Nancy Farmer's *The Sea of Trolls.* And yet the matings don't stop.

Two worlds. We can easily see this condition exemplified in the enmity and, later, the loving brotherhood of Gilgamesh—the urbane, the esteemed, the regent—and the bestial Enkidu. In even that earliest story, the doubleness is there. And in even that earliest story, we're given to see these two as the inescapable halves of a single being, as every one of us is: neocortex; brain stem. So with Jacob wrestling the angel: the conflict also occurs within himself. William Blake gives equal lyric urgency to his "Tyger" and his "Lamb." When the Martians land, will they be able to distinguish the everyday cops from the everyday robbers?

And Larona went to church on Sunday and dropped a dollar bill in the offering plate. And Larona turned a trick at Budget Room—a regular, he was easy, he got his nut off just by sucking her tits, and he gave her a pair of those dangly earrings she likes. And Larona took her sons to Walmart for their school supplies and to Foot Place for their start-of-the-school-year shoes, and then for ice cream. And Larona fucked Big T, and they did a blunt together, and then he gave her the leftover in a bag that

she could sell in the alley in back of Auto Inn to Rayray's sister, a bitch from Teeny's house she met at the after-party fighting two other bitches. And then she went home and fried up some chicken, and rearranged the living room plants.

In *The Prince and the Pauper,* the heir to the throne and the grubby ragamuffin boy, by trading places, trade—necessarily— cities, although the two cities involved are physically congruent. One is a city of privilege, manners, courtiers, gold-tined pheasant forks; one is a city of rats and gnawed bones. Each hears rumors of the other but can't believe it's true, not *really.* A hundred gazillion awareness-miles apart . . . but a single thing, to a map.

A few people knowingly hold dual citizenships: Larona is also Fantasee.

In the "buddy movie" the uptight starchy faithful-hubby CPA and the funky streetwise pussy-hungry hustler wind up jointly on the run from an international cartel of petrocriminals, and they learn to walk the walk of one another's normally insular worlds. Persephone is an alternating current: here-there, there-here. I don't have to point out that Jesus is half a human and half a deity, but he's only an extremo-mythic version of the story of *anybody's* twofold X and Y inheritance. Don't even get me *started* on Clark Kent/Superman. Or Nebuchadnezzar Masterson, the Civil War–era darkie who passed. Or the fifteenth-century Christian import merchant with his secret cellar for celebrating Hanukkah. *Two worlds.*

And Larona delivered trays of chocolate, vanilla, and strawberry cupcakes to the third-grade class of Anderson Elementary on her younger son's eighth birthday. And Larona got high and Larona spent two hours at the mirror doing her ho primp and Larona spritzed her coochie spray a final good-luck time, then did the bachelor party: guys lined up to see who'd lick the whipped cream off her nipples quickest, and she fucked the win-

ner for free and the other six took turns with cash in hand. And
Larona bought diapers and formula and baby aspirin at Cost-
Low. And Larona bought a Glock at E-Z Pawn—some bitches
was throwin' around some heavy shit.

And Larona was crazy, depressed and crazy, and crawl-
ing across the floor like a rabid dog and scratching the walls
and punching out a window, and Satin snuck the gun out of
the drawer. And Larona entered the club with her jilliondollar
boobs set high and her dangly earrings catching all of the party
wattage the ceiling had to dispense, and her plans for a Vegas
casino career were pulse-shimmering like an aurora around
her and she was beaming that easy from-the-sex-bone-on-up,
burn-you-with-its-radiation smile of hers, and *no one* on the
planet was as living a torch of human gung-ho endless hubba-
hubba fiery consummation as she was. "Fuck, you a *spuh-lit
personality*—I seen about it on television," Deezire said.

Okay. But it's also true that E-Z Pawn is only a block from
Anderson Elementary, and half of the people who fill their pre-
scriptions at Cost-Low also buy a bag or two in the alley in back
of Auto Inn. It isn't just that Larona is divided, but that the city
itself is a binary system.

And some people cross its median line a dozen times as a
day whirls around.

Larona tyger, Larona lamb.

And the men she fucked for money, who were Ted and John
and Richard, on occasion tried to jew her down, but many were
pleased to preen their sense of self (and of her worth) by throwing extra on the bed—she had her practiced ways to encourage
this—and the men she fucked for free, the ones who understood what she was about, who "got her," who were Cut-Eyes and
Dream and Up-Boy—oh they were fine and fun and hustler
jail-time baby daddies, so cool cool cool—they took her to their
clubs that were like shadows of the tony five-star restaurants that

Ted and John and Richard took her to—or was it the opposite, and did it matter? As David McCullough says, describing Paris in *The Greater Journey,* "Like all great cities, Paris was a composite of many worlds within, each going about its particular, preoccupying ways quite independent, or seemingly independent, of the others."

One phone rings: "Krystal here." And the other phone rings: Cost-Low saying her son's prescription asthma inhaler can be picked up.

2.

And Larona is Pashin. Jazmin. Baybee. Toy. Amour. A dozen different escort sites, a dozen steps ahead of a warrant, a creditor, a fist on the door at 6 a.m. Amanda. Lexie. Kreamy. Jewel. "As far as we can tell, the proteins of all life on Earth are made up of the same twenty amino acids." I read her that once. She thought "Amino" would be a terrific stripper name. "Don't park *there*. I'm 'Alana' there." And someone wrong was looking for Alana. An asshole. Samantha—someone right was trying to find Samantha, someone with an envelope he'd oh-so-subtly pass in a handshake. Mysti. Torie. Sapphire. Sunny. Princess. "God, I *hate* being bored!"

And what would popular culture do without the "secret identity"?

As early as 1837—forty-nine years ahead of Mr. Hyde titrating out of Dr. Jekyll—Robert Montgomery Bird creates a "dual identity" story, *Nick of the Woods,* featuring the protagonist's alter ego, the "Jibbenainosay." In 1869 the hero of Edward Ellis's prescient dime novel *The Phantom Horseman* turns, in a trance state, into that eponymous night-riding venturer. In 1905 the Baroness Emmuska Orczy creates Sir Percy Blakeney, "an effete popinjay" who disguises himself—in the interests of thrilling swordsmanship and hairbreadth escapes—as the dashing Scarlet Pimpernel, in the novel of the same name. Popular? Ten more novels about him followed.

Even as the idea of the bifurcated self is being explored in "serious literature" (Joseph Conrad's "The Secret Sharer," Virginia Woolf's *Orlando*), the pulp magazines of the twenties, thirties, and forties grow increasingly dependent upon this concept. Zorro ("the Fox," the "remarkable, mysterious avenging figure in black, who mete[s] out swift, unexpected justice with a deadly blade") is "really" Don Diego Vega, "something of a poetry-reading fop"; he debuts in 1919, in Johnston McCulley's

The Curse of Capistrano, a colonial-era-California remix of Orczy's Pimpernel. Meanwhile in a foggy, gaslit, noirish New York, Kent Allard "the famous aviator" roams his city's crime-ridden streets as that black-cloaked mystery figure the Shadow; his first magazine appearance is in April 1931, and the Shadow movies are still being ground out by Hollywood today.

The authors of certain pulp and paperback fictions turn out themselves to be as identity-twinned as any Wonder Woman or Hawkman:

> If Emil Richard Johnson's gritty, grim crime novels about crooks, killers, tough cops, and angry prisoners had a rare immediacy and a core of red-hot reality known to few other authors, it was no coincidence, and it didn't come cheap. . . . [He] was himself a convicted murderer and armed robber who spent most of his adult life behind bars and wrote nearly every page of his eleven mostly tough, dark works of fiction in the narrow confines of a cell at Stillwater State Prison in Minnesota.

Johnson's first published short stories were "sold to children's magazines."

In their prolific youth, such reliable wordaholics as Robert Silverberg, Lawrence Block, and Harlan Ellison churned out endless pseudonymous sleaze-o-rama titles, often under female pen names. Check out Silverberg's *Sin on Wheels* ("The Uncensored Confessions of a Trailer Park Tramp") by the gender-iffy Loren Beauchamp, or Richard E. Geis's *Beat Nymph,* with its byline, Peggy Swenson. (Geis was Peggy Swenson, Peggy Swanson, *and* Peggy Swan.) And women published as men: Marion Zimmer Bradley became John Dexter and Brian Morley—although for *Twilight Lovers* ("They Lived and Loved in the Off-Beat World of Lesbianism"), her name became Miriam Gardner. Shamelessly,

dozens of these subgenre workhorses masqueraded as medical practitioners, doing titillation books in the guise of studies on peeping-Tomism, nymphomania, various fetishes: Dr. So-and-So on whipping; Bullshit Blah Blah PhD on wife-swapping parties.

Perhaps the epitome of—and most complicated—doubling of doubling in pulp fiction's fantasy realms was Richard Wentworth's transformations from his fashionable life as a man of polo field and swank cabaret to his secret life as The Spider, Master of Men. That change alone was amazing: the crime fighter's misshaped face, small slip-in fangs, hunched walk, and eerie pallid cheeks were worlds away from Wentworth's days of well-tailored, untroubled leisure-class ease. Beyond that, however, The Spider himself was rarely The Spider: Richard Wentworth was "a master of disguise," and his trusted servant Ram Singh was the ultimate props-and-makeup man. "Wentworth maintained the meager little apartment under a fictitious name for the sole purpose of assuming his disguises when he secretly penetrated the underworld of New York City. A large closet in the bedroom was crammed with clothing, some of which would fit almost any character which Wentworth might wish to assume."

Why not? A man needs every edge he can get when battling The Cholera King or The Council of Evil or The Silver Terror, The Fire God, The Eyeless Legion, The Slaves of Hell, The Overlord of the Damned, The Gray Horde, The Vampire King, The Emperor of the Yellow Death, The King of the Fleshless Legion, The Sons of Satan, Murder's Black Prince . . . across nearly one hundred book-length adventures.

In *The Wheel of Death*, a girl named Molly is saved from demise at the hands of gangland goons by "a man with plastered hair and high-waisted trousers." His name is . . . "Any name," he says. "Try Dick." But "Dick" is Richard Wentworth, and Richard Wentworth is The Spider, and in a matter of pages he's neither: he's an eye-patched blind man, wrinkled of face and garb, and

Molly—they're off to rescue her father—is in ragged trousers se-
cured by a piece of twine, disguised as the urchin boy who leads
this nondescript blind man through the streets. Later, Wentworth
is "wearing full evening dress [embellished with] the rosette of
the Legion of Honor." Later still, he's grease-smeared by Ram
Singh, and in a "very dirty" coat that covers his evening dress
completely—he's a street bum! As for his girlfriend Nita Van
Sloan, well . . . under "the work of Ram Singh's nimble fingers . . .
her features changed and her face became flamboyant, painted
beyond the limits of a woman's oldest profession." If his fists
and his guns couldn't win the day, his strategy seems to have
been to *confuse* his enemies into submission.

So, it's in holistic keeping with this morphophilic character that Wentworth's writer Norvell Page (whose Spider author
name was the blander, "stock" Grant Stockbridge) could be
seen sometimes dressed up as The Spider, wearing his hero's
impressive black cape and wide-brimmed black hat, "roaming
up and down the sunny beaches of Florida resort town Ana
Maria"—a ligature of identities too impossible to *begin* to parse.

The switcheroo aesthetics of pulp creation couldn't even keep
astronomy inviolate. "Trying to avoid two stories set on the same
planet in the same issue . . . [Leigh] Brackett's editors once simply changed her title 'The Dragon Queen of Venus' to 'The
Dragon Queen of Jupiter.'" So I think of Larona's Sassy phone,
her Tasha phone, her "Hello, leave a message for Amber."
Cities change names—New York is Batman's Gotham, and is
Superman's Metropolis, and in Ed McBain's great-American-
novel 87th Precinct detective series it's called Isola. Larona the
wannabe PTA mom (not that she could even tell me what the
letters mean); Larona the pouter of pink, pink DSL—and this an
acronym she *could* explain: "dick-sucking-lips," she told me, with
an entrepreneurial pride one day. *Twenty amino acids* . . . and
look at the multi-selves in any one bar, on any one block, of any

one night in any one city that's *never* "one" city. "Good-bye, no Alana here."

"You're trouble, Larona. Trouble on six-inch stripper heels, you know that?"

"Oh, I know it. Trouble's my name."

"But you can't be trouble without then getting *in* trouble."

"Yeah, thass my other name."

My friend Brenda works in City Hall. She's up at seven every day, she packs the kids' school lunch bags, also Jerry's lunch (her husband of seventeen years is the business manager at Our Lady of the Valley Church), and she's at her desk at eight thirty, prompt; her desk is as neat as her dress is proper and tidy; her daily paperwork is prompt and proper and tidy; and she's home by eight, and in bed by ten—on weekends maybe eleven.

It's her signature that I see one afternoon on Larona's escorting license. Their paperwork moment of mutual fiscal business is a subatomic pinpoint where the bathwater that drains clockwise and the bathwater that drains counterclockwise touch—for those few moments—like the fingertips of beings from separate dimensions who breach the veil.

Her mother's name was Rhonda. Rhonda Wilson, who took out the "h" and the "d" and named her daughter Rona, then later Larona. (Long *o*—the *o* of pain and pleasure.) Whoever Wilson was, he'd left by then. But soon there was Carl, and then there was Ed and Tiger and Uncle Shelley . . . Some did this to her, and some did that, "but none of them saved for my college education, or bought me a birthday gift," and mostly what she remembers is fighting her brother to chew on the leftover bones—a younger brother . . . she'd usually intervene and volunteer to take the whippings he had coming—and her mother on crack, and her mother with johns, and her own tough years

of being passed like a football around the houses of foster care, and the always-burning-ever-hotter determination to never, *never,* EVER, be like her mother.

Larona was smarter than anybody else her age at the small-town drive-in and the roller rink, and maybe smarter than some of her diddly-squat downriver high school teachers. But she was born a crack baby: too impatient for a book or for a friendship. "I could fight, though. And the boys liked when I bent to pick something up." And in the military—she couldn't imagine any other option—she refined those abilities, on base learning the holds and lightning jabs that bring even a prizefighter down, and off base learning the holds men like. By the time she was discharged ("Honorably!") she had an out-of-wedlock child—and soon, a second—no job in sight, no training in how to find one.

"We lived in a car"—all three. "We'd wash up at the Kwik Shop out of paper cups. I made it a game, my sons thought it was fun, they didn't know no better." Every scrap she could scavenge was theirs; at last, in a loveless world, she'd been given two people to love—who loved her back, unquestioningly—and her heart discovered, and used up, its entire capability, by diving into the warm stream of her mama-self.

Somebody said she could make good money stripping. (Men were always stopping to feed her their clever suggestions.) "I'd never *been* in a strip club before. I didn't know *what* I was doing. All the girls had flashy outfits and there I was in my underwear." Her name was Stormy. Inside a week she was making more tips than anyone.

And some of the girls stepped out with a chosen customer for an hour. The sex was nothing: "I can marinate this pussy back tight in a ten-minute bath." The sex was nothing, the money was good, the kids were wearing designer jeans. And then the year at Diamond Girls, the escort agency. "Shit, why give *them* half? *They* aren't squirming around on their back." So then her life as an

independent escort, learning to build her own escort site. "I did it myself." She was Destiny. She was Sweetheart. Other girls in the business copied her.

In 2003, three hundred tax-free dollars an hour, three clients a day, added up to her own three-bedroom home, and private karate lessons for her sons, and lots and *lots* of weed. "Plus, some of them tipped an extra hundred or two." They *liked* impressing her. One client paid for her boob job; another, a couch; another, a day at a spa. "I'm like a celebrity!" They praised her—or some Majick or Sugar or Dominique version of her—online, on escort message boards. Her breasts and ass and glamorous eyes were the subject of fervent analysis and poetical flights. *Every toe is perfect,* they said.

Larona's red-eyed hissy fits over other girls in the game only heightened her star-status image: after all, aren't tabloid battlefests what spoiled celeb-queens *do?* And she was good at something—at last! She was good, and she was self-made, and her boys had all of the high-end sneakers they wanted, whether they wanted or not, and she rolled out of bed to her thongs-strewn floor and did herself up for work on any time clock of her own devising. She had no boss, unless vanity counts as a boss. She knew which eye shadow colors most flattered her, which bras pushed up and which pushed in and when they weren't needed; she knew which vaginal sponges worked best for absorptively hiding her period; she was a scientist and auteur artiste of calculated by-the-hour seduction. Her clients were "upscale men." Trial attorneys. Cardiac surgeons. Essentially, she was being paid to be worshipped. She'd found her calling.

But also the anger problems. Also being a bitch. "I know: I'm a bitch. I *love* being a bitch." It turns out that the more you're worshipped, the more you get to be a bitch. "But I'm a *hella fun* bitch!" Then immediately her laugh, which could turn a stone statue into malleable putty.

Also, it turns out, when you're a ho you live in a ho world. "One guy paid me a thousand dollars to go to the opera with him. I had a dress that I *almost* didn't spill out of. I didn't know what they were saying onstage, but I had this—what is it?" *Program?* "Yeah, I had this program, so I followed along. He was sweet, and he came just by seeing my body as soon as I wiggled out of my dress."

Later that night, with a thousand bucks and her *real* friends— her ho and pimp and dealer and food-stamp-scammer friends— *Don Giovanni* or *Madame Butterfly* or whatever it was, a distant memory floating on the farther side of a cloud of weed, and the *real* music, "Stick it in my face, bitch, Stick it in my face, bitch, Stick it in my face, bitch," over and over, the two huge speakers standing like sentries on either side of her living room door. The kids could sleep through any of it. The lies she required fell out of the sky like manna, directly onto her tongue. If she wanted a client, she answered the phone. If she didn't, she didn't. The Mozart city. The stick-it-in-my-face-bitch city.

Always the two.

I love those dark-mood movies and mystery novels in which the savvy schlep detective is hired for something mundane—to tail a pool shark's errant wife, let's say, or check on the opaque past of some suspicious widow's future daughter-in-law—and the sticky thread he discovers leads, by graduated and dangerful steps of inquiry, by bribe and call girl and jimmied lock, to revelations of murder, even betrayal of the nation's trust, in the halls of prestige and power. A sticky thread gets tugged in the dusk of a low-rent pool hall . . . and a senator topples.

In Daniel Woodrell's *Under the Bright Lights,* city councilman Alvin Rankin gets iced—it isn't pretty ("there were flecks of gray and chunks of white visible in the smears of red")—and Shade, the rough-around-the-edges-but-honest cop on the case,

is ordered that night to the mayor's house. I'm cutting and pasting, but basically this is the conversation:

"The burglars nowadays, Shade—what do you think, are they mostly junkies? This is one burglar I want caught in a hurry."

"I don't think this was a burglary. I think it was murder, straight up and simple."

"It could've been a burglar and Rankin surprised him."

"Not from the evidence," Shade said. "Nothing was taken from Rankin's house, and he was whacked while peeking at the tube with someone. Most people, when they surprise a burglar, don't ask what channel they want to watch."

"So you think Alvin Rankin was killed by someone close to him?"

"Yes, sir."

"And since he was a city councilman, maybe it all has something to do with that."

"Seems possible."

"What's the matter, Shade—don't you like politicians? You're a half-assed detective and I'm mayor. We get into a public pissing contest, who do you think the judges will favor?"

"Whoever got them appointed might get a few breaks."

That's page 44; 125 pages follow, in which the city of lowlife grifters—their hooker sometime-girlfriends, race fixers, drug runners, small-time assassins, and pimps—connects to the city of ancient Chinese vase collections and porcelain cups of tea. A thread, and Shade is there to tie it at both of its ends.

In the ancient Mesopotamian epic *Enuma Elish,* the son of the earth god, Marduk—in celebration of his victory over the

early forces of Chaos—founds the first great city, the center of which is a ziggurat that duplicates his shrine in the divine world. "As the symbol of 'infinite heaven' . . . it becomes the gods' earthly home. The city is called *'bab-ilani'* (the 'gate of the gods'), the place where the divine enters the world of men." Of course, thanks to the Bible the lustful (very *un*divine and naughty, haunting) image of "the whore of Babylon" enters our language, as does the very human idea of sorrow in captivity— and so the Jews in their bondage cry out, "By the rivers of Babylon, there we sat down, yea, we wept. . . . There they that carried us away captive required of us a song. . . . How shall we sing the Lord's song in a strange land?"

Thus it was in our species' primordial dwelling place, from which all others take their shape: the city of the gods, and the city of human sex and human tears, as mixed as when my mother used her set of clear-glass coffee cups and I'd witness the layer of cream on top of the bitter dark layer of coffee below, and she wouldn't stir for a minute, knowing how readily I was fascinated by watching the first descending pearly tentacles of the one become, at its own pace, in its dreamy shapes, indistinguishable from the other.

Is Larona white—or black? Is she twenty-two—or forty-two? I'm not saying. Let her quantum-mechanically blip from one state to another. Particle/wave. Ebony/blond. Pink-frosted ruby/brunette. And her real name isn't Larona Wilson. I'd never betray her like that.

3.

For the jot of a heartbeat Gilgamesh startles, up on the tower parapet where the priests convene to study the smoke of their sacrifices ascending to the heavens, and where they scan the patterns of wheeling stars for advice. He's climbed the stairs to this high place to think, and to believe, and to wrestle with serious questions, but . . . there, again . . . he feels the back of his brain rise in an animal sulk. It's Enkidu-him, his Other, that won't ever leave completely.

Or is it Enkidu who startles up from a day of running on all fours with the lions of the hills, and rutting, and slopping up green pond water with his tongue . . . but an itch, a glow, in his head . . . suddenly his Gilgamesh-him is alive, and he aspires to something exalted he hasn't the words for.

And so the brother (or sister) is always here—so close that by "here" I mean deeply subcutaneous. And if we need an exterior correlative to symbolize this, we couldn't do better than all of those unofficial stories of twins, in which the one on the East Coast wakes up—panting, panicked, forehead under a bunting of sweat—at exactly the minute ("I checked my watch!") her sister on the West Coast, in a back-road stand of timber, is attacked by a mad-eyed bear.

Or maybe more forcefully, the official story of Giovanni and Giacomo Tocci, dicephalous conjoined twins born in Locana, Italy, in 1877: the single organism "had two heads, two necks and four perfect arms, but only one lower body and one pair of legs"—"two distinct individuals" genetically bundled as one. The chest held two separate hearts and separate pairs of lungs. "Each child could see, hear, feel, think, eat, drink, and cry, and their mental activity was completely independent."

And you're wondering now, so I'll tell you: the brothers shared a single anus and single set of genitals—though in 1904, at age twenty-seven, after lives spent touring as the world's most

highly paid sideshow freaks, the brothers retired, "bought a pretty little villa in Venice," and "married two separate women." One hopes that their domestic lives were contented, although I'm taken by this *New York Truth* report in 1892: "When one of the heads is sleepy, the other is wakeful and prevents any attempt at slumber. When one stomach craves food, the other repels it. When one is jolly and playful, the other is morose and sullen. In fact, Tocci has a hard time of it with himself."

And what would The Novel do without the time-honored theme of sibling-love-cum-sibling-rivalry? In *Under the Bright Lights,* Shade is Rene Shade, cop and protagonist. Yes, but the truculent thug bar owner is his brother Tip Shade, and the all-too-power-hungry schemer and dandy from the DA's office is brother Francois Shade, and their triangulated conflictedness is one of the engines that makes this story run. But think about Cain and Abel: families have *forever* been conflicted.

We can see this idea written large in the public records of a typical medieval village. In Elton in the English East Midlands, most of the well-known families "who were active in public service" were landholders. "Four members of the In Angulo family accounted for a total of fourteen offices"—jurors, beadles, reeves. In all, between 1279 and 1342, four families provided over thirty public officials, many repeating their service year after year. These would all have been the respectable (and well-connected) village elite; their counterparts today would live in the best of gated communities and receive free parking at football games.

"That these same families also figure prominently in the court rolls for quarrels, suits, infractions, and acts of violence is a striking fact." (Though not, perhaps, a surprising one.) In 1294 Roger Goscelin "drew blood from Richer Chapelyn" and two of the In Angulo wives "did hamsoken" another woman—i.e., assaulted her in her own house. Richard Beynt, two times

a juror, "badly beat Thomas Clerk and did hamsoken upon him." But Richard Beynt did not escape from this vale of tears unscathed: in 1306 John Ketel "did hamsoken upon him" (and also "broke the head" of Nicholas son of Richard Smith). Bar brawls. Adultery. Knife attacks. In 1303 Matilda daughter of John Abovebrook, in 1307 Athelina Blakeman, in 1312 Alice daughter of Robert atte Cross, in 1306 both Alice and Muriel of the In Angulos . . . all "were convicted of 'fornication.'"

Rene Shade is savvy enough to know that there's no uniformly equal crowd of drinkers in his brother Tip's bar; someone's uncle is someone else's out-on-bail hit man. "The bar was the center of the neighborhood in which they had grown up, and the regulars were neighbors first and threats to society second. It was not all clear-cut, where the line could, or even should, be drawn." Closing time: 25 people leave. But that's only a number. Subjectively 50, 100, maybe 250 people leave. It's the city: some belong to a gang. But *everybody*—cop, pickpocket, you—belongs to a doppelgang.

The city: like "fish," it's also a plural.

The city: spuh-lit personality.

You can't win with Larona.

1. "I'm considering going to law school." "Larona, I've never even seen a fucking *TV Guide* in your house. I've never seen you stop to read a *fridge magnet*." And then the Look—her specialty—that could wither entire gardens' worth of vegetables.

2. Larona parks in back so she can't be seen from the street. Larona has her car windows tinted (illegally dark) "'cause my business, see, is *my* business." Larona always takes "the back roads" on the simplest one-mile Kwik Shop trip. Cautious. Private. "But then, Larona, your vanity plate screams TAYSTEE." The Look.

3. "I'm smart and I'm hot and I don't *need* a pimp, and I never had NO PIMP!" (This said with her own inflated—and

justified—version of pride in being a self-made and successful businesswoman.) But when her piece-of-shit hustler boyfriend Stik or Mover or Delron feels like beating her up and leaving with her jewelry or money, not the Glock and not the baseball bat and not the pink box cutter in her ho purse can prevent it. "Larona, the *whole world's* your pimp." The Look to a factor of ten. And then—that laugh, that jolly jiggle of her goods, that would make a dead man smile. That guileless-but-piratical laugh.

You can't win with Larona. But then, she's too alive for this sorry-ass world, and Larona can't win with Larona either.

The last time Stik went at her—in fact, the last time Stik did *anything* on the outer side of jail bars—they were over at Teebone's cousin's, drunk, and he used his fists on her face (her treasure!), her boobs (her fortune!), her ribs (one broke), and a neighbor thought she saw a gun and she called the police, and both Larona and Stik were taken in (just tell *the cops* Stik wasn't her pimp—uh-huh), and they questioned her overnight, and they called her a whore and slapped her around a little and threw her cell phone against the wall and told her if she didn't turn state's evidence against Stik she would never see her goddam children again, and even as they were saying this monstrous thing a squad car was parked at her house, where as it happened the babysitter—Honey, the seventeen-year-old slut—had abandoned the kids to go fuck her boyfriend E-Jay, which made it look as if *Larona* had abandoned the kids (but she hadn't, she'd hired a babysitter!), and Social Services got involved, and the boys were taken into the state, the system, the legal suckhole . . . her boys, her heart, her only love was gone, her only-thing-to-live-for.

It depends on who you ask, but many cultures will swear that the djinn live among us—invisible, but there as surely as you or I. The census won't account for them, they'll never be tapped

for jury duty, but they're a population interpenetrating right now with your family, your colleagues, your afternoon traffic jam. That sound when there's no wind? Your missing [fill in the blank]? The djinn. And other people have said that *everything* has a soul—a rock, a rock soul; a lettuce, a lettuce soul; a ring of keys is a little soul family jingling. Imagine a city like that; imagine the size and heft of its soul census report.

And the ancestors won't let go of the physical planet: every year, they're brought their offering bowls of rice (a gift? a bribe?) and their counsel is earnestly solicited (for most of them, more respectfully than ever sought out in life), and for a night they walk (or float, or hazily teleport) through the everyday avenues all of us use on our way to work or sex or prayer or a couple of drinks between. The faeries normally keep to their grassy rings, but everyone knows that at night sometimes they'll creep across the border, staying inside the shadows but making their way as if the shadows were stepping-stones, and they'll leave their presents or work their mischiefs right at our front-door stoops. A man in line with you at the bank is blankly bland but is also the Great Gazoo of the Mystic Order of Prairie Knights. You wouldn't know by her unremarkable surface, but the woman in charge of canned goods up at Cost-Low has the country's largest collection of ceramic state-themed thimbles. The largest ever: she has a document. I've seen a drunk Larona with her ho friends lift her glass in a toast: "Married to the Game!"—by which they meant a full immersion in their off-the-charts and under-the-radar adrenaline-pumping outsider lives that serve as their greatest devotion—and they fill their cars with gas and buy their baby diapers like anyone. And somebody else is married to Christ, and converses with him. And somebody else converses with her husband seven years after seeing him lowered into the grave.

I can't attest to the faeries or djinn, but the cockroaches

think that this is *their* city. There are more of them than us, they're perfectly comfortable in their million-branching scuttle-ways, and *we're* the ghosts or the gods or the monsters they sense as cohabiting presence.

So began Larona's decline. *I'd* say decline, but she might see it as only another tough-luck interim downslope detour on a sly and courageous survivor's journey toward (one day, maybe) triumph—and if not triumph, then a bearably enjoyable day-to-day "getting by." But the children were what kept her human, here on the side of the line with the rest of us. She looked in the mirror one morning and saw *her* mother.

Oh, she fought the court's decision. She *loved* those two boys in the nuclei in the cells in every fiber of her psyche, and she fought it. She worked to hide or transform the "who" of herself in compliance with this mission; she took the anger class and the parenting course and the endless demeaning pee and follicle drug tests. ("It costs forty-five dollars, but Zee swears *this* shampoo will erase it outta my hair!") She blotted her I'm-for-sale ads off the Internet, she punched holes into her house's wall in private so that she didn't need to punch anyone in a parking lot, she fought it, she drank (but not before a pee test), and she got high (ditto) and talked trash and delighted still in swinging her hips in her spray-on jeans around the cosmos of goggle-eyed men, but all that time what she really was doing was fighting it: she went to court, she did her lawyer visits, she went to court again, and again; she fought it as determinedly and drainingly and vociferously as any mother could, and she lost . . . of course. She could win over any man's dick but not the judge's pre-determined legalistic mind; she wasn't made for *that* justice.

And she reached her own ground zero one day in the lobby of Social Services—the notice they'd served her asked for "routine update"—when she thunderstormed out of the conference

room and stood there alone in that public space, surrounded by strangers, a column of flame (as she always was) five-foot-six with legs that went on for miles, and fuming imperiously with an anger that could have cracked aircraft in half. She raised her arm in the air like a queen declaiming to an enemy host, "Fuck you fuck you fuck you ALL!" in a decibel shrillness that traveled from her gut to the moon, until they roughly ushered her out. In the car she was silent a long half hour. And then— every word like a separate bullet—"I. Thought. That. I. Erased. It. All. But. They. Dug. Up. A. Year. Old. Escort. Site. I WILL *NEVER . . .* SEE MY CHILDREN . . . *AGAIN.*" Well, that escort site had been their hot dogs, vitamin pills, and the Spider-Man alarm clock to rouse them each morning for school.

She was left with a thinned-out client list. Her car was impounded. Rayray drove her out of state to turn a few tricks and have some fun; he beat her and took her money, and when the cops came she had some weed in her pocket. (He had way worse.) Vanna let her sleep on the couch. Vanna was a bitch, fuck Vanna. All of the ancient grievances, like bits of glass taken into her body in childhood, were rising back to the surface: "If you don't give me some money NOW, you gonna find your car in parts!" Lola let her sleep on the couch. Fooboy's baby momma was jealous and hit her with a brick. She pawned her jewelry. Lola's boyfriend stole her purse—good-bye to cell phone and ID—but P-Shady said he'd get it back. Brianna let her sleep on the couch. Shrieking through the neighbor's wall: "I'll get you one day, bitch, I can wait!" Larona's voice? Brianna's? Some said Extasee's. (Did it matter?) And then the world lost track of her. Life goes on. There are books and dental appointments. Hair gets cut and engines get oiled. Months went by, then more months.

Just recently, though, maybe 9:00 p.m. in the supermarket lot, I heard a honk. "Hey, don't you say hello?" Miss Cee was letting

her sleep on the couch, and the car she was driving (or that's the way the story went) was Miss Cee's. Through the bruises on her face, she still looked radiant, still gave out the old acetylene gusto. No, she didn't have any money or a phone of her own right now, but she was "getting things together." She was "taking it easy." Things were "about to happen." She had connections. Everyone liked her. The casino job in Vegas was hers whenever she could afford to get her ass out there. The kids would "always be mine" *wherever* they were. She wouldn't stop now and she wouldn't stop ever.

And I remembered reading about the cave some hikers unexpectedly came across in a cliff face sixty feet above the sea near Arbroath, Scotland—they'd seen a rope ladder bolted to the rock and climbed down it. The cave had been sealed off and "the whole of the front had been sprayed with insulation foam, which had then been painted to match the color of the rocks." And more: "The cave had a well-laid plywood floor screwed to solid wooden joists. To one side was a double seat taken from a bus, immaculate in its red fake leather covering. Strewn around were several beer cans, a red carpet, a blue jersey, and some artfully arranged tea lights. A number of short, heavy chains were embedded in the rock, their purpose unclear. Some of the walls were painted. Nobody was home." No one in the area even knew of its existence, nor who had created this hidden inner-world haven.

It never stops. Another story from what I call the looniverse. Above, or to the side of us, or underground, are other lives, each as dear and combustible and implacable as our own.

McCullough's *The Greater Journey* chronicles the adventures of those first early nineteenth-century Americans who explored their passions (literary, artistic, medical) in Paris. Nathaniel Willis went as a roving correspondent for the *New-York Mirror*.

"Having spent his first week walking the city in drizzling rain, [he] said that when the sun burst forth at last it so changed all his previous impressions that he had to set off and see it all a second time. 'And it seemed to me another city,' he wrote. 'I never realized so forcibly the beauty of sunshine.'"

"When I'm in Vegas and rich, I'm having a chauffeur and a personal chef. *That* city gonna be *good* to me!"

Missy. Shampane. Erotika. Bree . . .

SOURCES

The Adventures of Form and Content, on nearly every page, is informed by, and so indebted to, a crazy-quilt personal library of readings—from entire books like (this is only one of many examples) Mary Douglas's *Purity and Danger,* to small sidebars in an ever-branching, sloughing, accreting community of magazines and newspapers (or, often enough, to what became my notes from those sources, scribbled for a decade and a half onto the backs of receipts and on napkins, and now about as gone with the wind as Margaret Mitchell's fabular pre–Civil War Savannah). Given the length of time involved, and the untrackable flurry of sticky notes and scrawled-on bookmarks and clippings involved, some of the credit I should give to inspiring sources must remain implicit.

Of the journals that originally published these essays, three (the *Gettysburg Review,* the *Iowa Review,* the *Southern Review*) chose not to use a list of acknowledged sources. Gone, gone, gone with the wind. What follows is a combined list of acknowledged sources for two of the three essays that originally appeared in the *Georgia Review.* Some of my background reading, of course, even when it isn't part of the following list, is acknowledged by title and/or author within the text of the essays themselves.

On a few occasions, material even within quotation marks bears small changes for the purposes of concision or rhythm

(never for content). Any errors of fact or onslaughts upon sensibility?—aim brickbats at me, not at the following.

"Everybody's Nickname"
Mike Benton, *The Comic Book in America: An Illustrated History; Bud Plant's Incredible Catalog* (Summer 2006); James A. Corrick, *Double Your Pleasure: ACE S.F. Doubles;* Gustav Eckstein, *The Body Has a Head; Fortean Times* (number 211); Albert Goldbarth, various memories (both true and false) and earlier essays; James Gunn, *Alternate Worlds: The Illustrated History of Science Fiction;* Christine Kenneally, "The Deepest Cut" (the *New Yorker*); Richard A. Lupoff, *The Great American Paperback: An Illustrated Tribute to Legends of the Book;* Carl Sagan, *Broca's Brain: Reflections on the Romance of Science;* Piet Schreuders, *The Book of Paperbacks;* Lee Server, *Over My Dead Body; Wichita Eagle,* various editions, June 20–29, 2006; Betsy Wollheim, "The Family Trade" *(Locus).*

"A Cave in a Cliff in Scotland"
Anonymous, "The Devil's Head Cave" *(Fortean Times);* Anonymous, "New Protein Drugs Might Be Supernatural" *(Cosmos);* Karen Armstrong, *A Short History of Myth;* Jan Bondeson, "On Tour with the Tocci Twins" *(Fortean Times);* Nancy Farmer, *The Sea of Trolls;* Frances and Joseph Gies, *Life in a Medieval Village;* Gary Lovisi, *Dames, Dolls & Delinquents: A Collector's Guide to Sexy Pulp Fiction Paperbacks;* David McCullough, *The Greater Journey: Americans in Paris;* Joseph Rainone, *Art & History of American Popular Fiction Series,* vol. 1; Lee Server, *Encyclopedia of Pulp Fiction Writers;* Grant Stockbridge, *The Wheel of Death;* Daniel Woodrell, *Under the Bright Lights.*

In an early book of poems I used, as an epigraph, the following quotation from Kenneth Grahame's *The Reluctant Dragon,* and it seems worth reusing here: "What the boy chiefly dabbled

in was natural history and fairy tales, and he just took them as they came, in a sandwichy sort of way, without making any distinctions; and really his course of reading strikes one as rather sensible." And a speaker in Sean Russell's novel *The Compass of the Soul:* "The story you told us that night . . . the meaning was clear, the emotional truth there for anyone to hear. The facts . . . the facts should not be mistaken for truth."

ACKNOWLEDGMENTS

The essays in this collection were originally published by the following, and gratitude is extended to the editors involved.

"Everybody's Nickname": *The Georgia Review*
"Roman Erotic Poetry": *The Gettysburg Review*
"A Cave in a Cliff in Scotland": *The Georgia Review*

Additionally:

"Everybody's Nickname" was anthologized in *The Best American Essays;*

"Roman Erotic Poetry" was anthologized in *The Pushcart Prize* and appeared in a small-press edition from Essay Press;

"A Cave in a Cliff in Scotland" received the Gold Award for Best Essay of the Year from the Magazine Association of the Southeast.

Thanks to Jeff and Katie and the rest of the Graywolf Press family, for more reasons than I can say here. And Kyle too: the Dean of Cover Design. / As always, this book is for Skyler. / No computer was used in the research for, writing of, or submission of these essays.

ALBERT GOLDBARTH has been publishing books of note for over forty years, including *The Kitchen Sink: New and Selected Poems, 1972–2007,* which was a finalist for the *Los Angeles Times* Book Prize and received the Binghamton University Milt Kessler Award. Among other honors, he has twice won the National Book Critics Circle Award in poetry, and has received a Guggenheim Fellowship, three fellowships from the National Endowment for the Arts, and the Poetry Foundation's Mark Twain Award. Goldbarth is the author of five collections of essays, including *Many Circles: New and Selected Essays,* and a novel, *Pieces of Payne.* He lives in Wichita, Kansas.

The text of *The Adventures of Form and Content* is set in Baskerville, a typeface designed by John Baskerville in the 1750s and cut by John Handy. Book design by Ann Sudmeier. Composition by Bookmobile Design & Digital Publisher Services, Minneapolis, Minnesota. Manufactured by Versa Press on acid-free, 30 percent postconsumer wastepaper.

Graywolf Press

There are a lot more
where this one came from!

Like what you read in *The Adventures of Form and Content*?
We have many exciting titles of fiction, nonfiction, and poetry
inexpensively priced in handsome editions essential for your
home library or collection. Now you can read all the books
you have always wanted to in affordable editions and
with unparalleled literary quality.

Download your FREE catalog of Graywolf Press books now and
find out more about how YOU can be a part of it all at:

www.graywolfpress.org

Graywolf Press • 250 Third Avenue North, Suite 600 • Minneapolis, MN 55401

The text of *The Adventures of Form and Content* is set in Baskerville, a typeface designed by John Baskerville in the 1750s and cut by John Handy. Book design by Ann Sudmeier. Composition by Bookmobile Design & Digital Publisher Services, Minneapolis, Minnesota. Manufactured by Versa Press on acid-free, 30 percent postconsumer wastepaper.

ALBERT GOLDBARTH has been publishing books of note for over forty years, including *The Kitchen Sink: New and Selected Poems, 1972–2007,* which was a finalist for the *Los Angeles Times* Book Prize and received the Binghamton University Milt Kessler Award. Among other honors, he has twice won the National Book Critics Circle Award in poetry, and has received a Guggenheim Fellowship, three fellowships from the National Endowment for the Arts, and the Poetry Foundation's Mark Twain Award. Goldbarth is the author of five collections of essays, including *Many Circles: New and Selected Essays,* and a novel, *Pieces of Payne.* He lives in Wichita, Kansas.

ACKNOWLEDGMENTS

The essays in this collection were originally published by the following, and gratitude is extended to the editors involved.

"Annals of Absence": *Southern Review*

"Wuramon": *Iowa Review*

"Two Characters in Search of an Essay": *Georgia Review*

"The End of Space": Tavern Books

Additionally:

"Annals of Absence" was reprinted online at *Poetry Daily;* and "Wuramon" appeared in a small-press edition from Essay Press.

Thanks to Jeff and Katie and the rest of the Graywolf Press family, for more reasons than I can say here. And Kyle too: the Dean of Cover Design. / As always, this book is for Skyler. / No computer was used in the research for, writing of, or submission of these essays.